The Helmsley Chronicles

Michele

The Helmsley Chronicles

A diary celebrating rural and church life …
a remedy for the uncertainties of the
modern world

David Wilbourne

With all good wishes

+David Wilbourne

DARTON · LONGMAN + TODD

First published in Great Britain in 2012 by
Darton, Longman and Todd Ltd
1 Spencer Court
140 – 142 Wandsworth High Street
London
SW18 4JJ

ISBN: 978-0-232-52894-7

A catalogue record for this book is available from the British Library.

The author and the publishers would like to thank Gwydion Thomas of the
R. S. Thomas estate for permission to reproduce the extract from *Residues*
by R. S. Thomas (Bloodaxe Books, 2002).

Phototypeset by Kerrypress Ltd, Luton, Bedfordshire
Printed and bound by ScandBook AB

The Helmsley Chronicles is dedicated to our daughters, Ruth, Hannah and Clare, for bringing us all such cheer.

Contents

Part One

1997

❧ *Thursday, 1st May*

I cycled down to the primary school-cum-polling station and voted, the bright Mayday sunshine compounding the air of utter optimism. I hummed 'Things can only get better' as I pedalled into York along the snaking River Ouse, past Terry's chocolate factory belching out delicious aromas, a chocolate box in every breath. I dodged numerous tourists as I rode through the city, Whip-Ma-Whop-Ma-Gate packed to the hyphens. I sped past the majestic Minster, where both my dad and I had been ordained decades back, parking my bike by the Purey Cust's stone wall, careful not to scratch the Mercs and Jaguars jammed into this private hospital's car park.

The matron greeted me warmly. The last time I had seen her was when we had used the top floor of the hospital as a vestry for Archbishop David Hope's enthronement just over a year before. Peter Tatchell had threatened to disrupt proceedings, so Special Branch had singled out the hospital as a base whose security they could guarantee. Each of York Diocese's bishops had been given a whole ward to robe in, and then had descended en masse in their coped and mitred splendour in the lift. They emerged opposite the operating theatre, only to terrify some poor soul who was just being wheeled out, who must have thought he was having the strangest glimpse of heaven. 'We told him it was just the after-effects of the morphine,' Matron laughed as we recalled the event. 'Now let me take you to Lord Feversham.'

A ruddy-faced Lord Feversham was sitting up in bed, a linen tent over his gammy leg. 'I'm sorry about your leg, sir,' I began. But my studied pastoral concern was dismissed by a wave of a hand which had all the chill of Henry VIII about it. 'Don't worry about that, boy, it'll heal like it's healed before. But there's been some rum goings on at Helmsley, what with our vicar and his mistress appearing *in flagrante delicto* in the *News of the World* on Easter Day, of all days. Nor have we been helped by you lot at the Diocese fining us a couple o' thousand for nailing a few Stations of the Cross to the wall. What are you going to do about it?'

'Well, I'd like to come and be your vicar, get things running smoothly again,' I replied, my brusque matching his.

'You mean like Martin Bell's going to sort out Tatton after the Hamiltons – providing, of course, he gets elected? Have you voted yet?'

'Yes.'

'Who did you vote for?' Clearly this guy wasn't afraid of straight talking.

'I voted New Labour,' I admitted shyly, 'although I'm actually a Bennite.'

'Good for you. They screened *Brassed Off* at Helmsley's little cinema last night – I heard there wasn't a dry eye in the place, so Labour'll romp home for sure. But Tony Benn's a queer old stick, yet talks a lot of good sense. Though why he gave up his seat in the House of Lords defeats me. But enough of politics; you want me to vote you in as our new vicar?'

'Well, as patron yours is the only vote that counts.'

He suddenly winced with pain. 'No need to flatter me,' he said gruffly. 'So what have you got to offer us? What's your manifesto?' Lord Feversham chuckled at his own election-day joke, a fiendish chuckle worthy of a Henry VIII-cum-Herod.

'I know the Church of England, the Diocese of York, Helmsley like the back of my hand. I'd get you running on the right tracks again, but with a bit of oomph thrown in.'

'What do you think of the Book of Common Prayer?' The questions were coming staccato fashion, but I was ready for them.

'I've known it since I was a boy. It's a book with some beautiful words, but useless as a tool for evangelism and mission.'

'I'm not sure the folk of Helmsley will agree with you about the last bit.'

'Well, read the BCP Epistle for Trinity 13 out to them, with all that seed and not seeds stuff, and ask any of them listening to make any sense of it whatsoever!'

'I couldn't agree more, some bits of it are total gobbledegook! But the last bloke promised to use nothing but the BCP, and then hardly ever used the thing. What do you promise?'

'That I will use only the forms of worship permitted by Canon.'

The ward filled with gales of lordly laughter. 'You're a slippery sod – ever thought of a career in politics? No, don't answer that! What's your view of Remembrance Sunday? Last bloke upset 'em all.'

'I think there's still a lot of wounds, a lot of hurt memories around, and our job is to heal them and move people on.'

'Fair enough. And what about all this high church business? I think we've gone too extreme at Helmsley – all these bells and smells are putting folk off.'

'I think a lot of Catholic ritual brings drama and colour to worship, but I can't be doing with all the excesses, which seem nonsense.'

'Couldn't agree more! Lady Feversham is a Roman Catholic and she claims our church faffs around over the ritual more than hers.' Suddenly Lord Feversham looked at his watch. 'Right, I'll ring for lunch. You can pedal back to Bishopthorpe and tell the Archbishop you'll do.' I was summarily dismissed and appointed in one fell swoop.

As I cycled home, I recalled the advert Lord Feversham had placed in the *Church Times*, when the parish was vacant three years before, following the death of the elderly incumbent who'd become vicar there in the year I'd been born. The blurb accompanying the advert bizarrely included the following comment: 'How wise of the previous vicar not to shake hands at the church door following a service. Of shaking hands inside the church, we will not speak.' It reminded me of the fiercely conservative Wolds parish, where the churchwarden had angrily scored through each section in the modern communion service where the Peace is shared, writing in red, 'THERE IS NO PEACE, HERE!' I suspected bringing peace to Helmsley wasn't going to be the easiest of jobs. But surely, things could only get better ...

🍂 Thursday, 28th August

Helmsley nestles at the southern edge of the North York Moors, 30 miles north of York. Though it can be reached from every compass point, on our moving-in day we choose the spectacular approach from the west, across the Vale of Mowbray, the low point, the hated flatlands of Wainwright's *Coast to Coast* walk. Driving through James Herriot's Thirsk on the A170, a veritable mountain range looms to the east. 'We must climb that one day,' a stranger might think, little realising that his stuttering car will have to climb it today, as the road snakes up the infamous Sutton Bank, with a 1:4 gradient and hairpin bends for mile after mile. The car's temperature gauge swings perilously close to the red zone as it mercifully reaches the top. We gasp as we look at Yorkshire in all its panorama, the Dales, the Pennines, the industrial west and south, with York Minster, just a toy church from this distance, mediating between us and the cooling towers belching out their toxic vapours, bound for Scandinavia with our love. Often in winter while the rest of Yorkshire is green, Sutton Bank's top surprises you with a couple of feet of snow.

Having made the peak, our car gradually descends for eight miles, until we round a bend and Helmsley lies beneath us, its red roofs huddled around the silver River Rye, with the dark shadow of the bleak moors its backdrop. The place used to be called Helmsley Blackamoor; Helmsley Back o' Moors might have been more appropriate. Racing down the steep hill I feel more like a fighter pilot than a car driver, zooming in to land, the bustling market and the Black Swan hotel flying past before we come to rest at Canons Garth, Helmsley's Vicarage, adjacent to the parish church, our home for the next eleven years.

🍂 *Sunday, 31st August*

Woke up to hear the news that Princess Diana has been killed in a car crash in Paris. 'Oh well, that's that then,' I thought. How wrong could I be! As we unpack box after box in the living room, we watch the unfolding news on the TV. It's all driven by the media as it covers Tony Blair's 'impromptu' speech outside his parish church in nearby Sedgefield, then switching to Buckingham Palace with sweet little girl after sweet little girl bringing flowers to prop up against the railings.

On 8 December 1992, my then boss, Archbishop Habgood, gave the slightest hint that something really, really big was coming up the following day. He then sped off to London to be present as the Primate of England for an announcement in the Houses of Parliament. I was convinced that we were going to declare war on God knows who, so sent Rachel off to Tesco to stockpile cans of corned beef, only to find the announcement was John Major giving notice of Charles and Diana's separation. John Habgood came back from London looking drawn. 'Diana's playing a very funny game!' was his only comment. Not as funny as the game we had to play, consuming tin upon tin of corned beef for the next six weeks.

Next May I accompanied my boss to Liverpool Cathedral for the Battle of the Atlantic service, also attended by Prince

Charles and Princess Diana. They had precedence and a mere Archbishop and his chaplain stood behind them for the military walk-past outside the cathedral. It was a windy day and Princess Diana's skirt flew up in a gale, her dress quickly adjusted by prim ladies-in-waiting and slightly over keen equerries. My boss caught my gaze with a distinct twinkle in his eye: we had suddenly joined that select number of males who had seen Di's pants!

BBC News is going out around the clock, as if it were election night, with shot after shot of the flowers outside Buckingham Palace, by now a veritable mountain of multi-coloured blooms. Diana's 'funny game' clearly continues post-mortem. I break off watching the TV and unpacking to deal with a tramp who wants to borrow a fiver to tide him over until the banks open tomorrow.

🖋 *Tuesday, 2nd September*

I watched Ruth, our 11-year-old daughter, get on the school bus for the first time. I was a clucking hen, checking my chick crossed the road and got on the bus safely; Ruth, almost grown-up and going to Big School, understandably didn't want father fussing and spoiling her street-cred. So like God, I watched at a distance, thinking on the poet C. Day Lewis' great line, 'Selfhood begins with a walking away, love is proved in the letting go.'

I guess I was a bit jumpy because I recalled all too well the school bus from my own primary school days in the 1960s. We lived in the middle of nowhere and the bus, built in 1929, was driven by a guy who had been injured by a heavy iron triangle falling on his head in the bus garage and was near-blind. The driver clearly knew the route by heart, and was aided by Jimmy, the biggest boy in the school, sitting next to him and grabbing the steering wheel should the bus suddenly veer to one side or other. Jimmy's assistance wasn't always appreciated however, and we were often treated to an outburst of bad language from the disgruntled driver. Fortunately there weren't that many cars around in those days, and all the locals were in the know and made sure their cars weren't parked on the road at school-run times. Then was clearly a different age in terms of health and safety.

Snapping back to the present, I noticed that instead of piling onto the bus like a scrum, the crowd of Helmsley children were incredibly courteous, politely queuing in an orderly manner, letting the little ones go on first. Soon the albeit ancient bus, with a mercifully fully sighted driver, disappeared leaving just a blue pall of smoke hovering over the market place.

It was my first day at the nearby Ryedale Comprehensive School too, in that I had arranged to take assembly, with strict instructions from Ruth not even to hint that there was any connection between the two of us. I cycled to the school, which is some three miles equidistant from Helmsley and its neighbouring market town of Kirkbymoorside. It was built there in 1952 so that children could travel to it by train on the little branch line which ran along the southern edge of the North York Moors, a cunning plan sadly to be thwarted when the branch line closed a year later. The pupils now reached the isolated school by bus, taxi or private car, and once they had arrived in the morning, they were there for the day, with nowhere else to go, other than the surrounding green fields and woods which ran on for miles.

This gave the place a sense that, since this was definitely the only show in town, the show just had to be a good one. When I was the Archbishop of York's chaplain, as part of the archiepiscopal roadshow, I'd previously visited the school and we were much impressed by its family feel and high expectations. Today I was similarly impressed, with a headteacher who was hands-on, who clearly believed in managing by walking around on the shop floor rather than cowering out of sight in his office. We stood together at the hall door as the pupils filed in for assembly; Ruth gave me a shy smile and then looked away. The Head seemed to know nearly all the children by name, even the new ones, pulling them up short if their ties were loose or their shirts untucked (neither seemed heinous crimes in my book). When all were gathered in, every pupil stood as the Head and I marched down the hall aisle and strode onto the stage. Last night's news had featured a gay wedding in America, where two butch men had walked proudly down the aisle; I kept my distance from the Head, just in case any mischievous teenager should strike up 'Here comes the bride!' Given the strong sense of discipline, I don't think anyone would have dared.

My talk was routine stuff. I got the new pupils to engage with a bit of mental maths to calculate (eventually!) that the earth would travel more than 30,000 million miles during their time at the school. I quoted Cardinal Basil Hume, formerly Abbot of nearby Ampleforth Abbey, who defined his job as coming to where people were and taking them to places they never dreamt of going. Just as they never dreamt of travelling 30,000 million miles during their time at Ryedale, the distance travelled in terms of their own development, learning and faith would be similarly mind-boggling. I encouraged them simply to be open to journeying, with their teachers, me and God cast as fellow travellers.

As I say, routine stuff. Unlike the elderly woman priest who began her albeit well-intended assembly at an inner-city comprehensive by holding up a banana and naively encouraging the pupils to shout any abusive words at it that sprang to mind. The normally reticent pupils rose as one to her invitation, much to the embarrassment and frustration of the teachers present.

Her assembly involved piercing the banana's skin beforehand with a needle and effectively performing key-hole surgery to slice the soft interior. Having allowed the banana to be insulted, you then examine it from the outside and notice nothing amiss, before peeling it to check all is OK. Which is when you discover that it is all cut up on the inside. Moral: calling people names cuts them up on the inside. Tip for anyone using that assembly: prepare cards with appropriate insults for people to shout out, such as 'yellow', 'spotty' or 'bent', to spare you a torrent of words more colourful than my school bus driver regaled us with when Jimmy grabbed the wheel.

Following my assembly, I watched a fierce head of lower school barking at the children to stack their chairs – how many times have I led assemblies whose theme was the love of God for all his valued children, only to have the rug pulled from under me by a member of staff treating a child like dirt and tearing a strip off them? We had only been in Helmsley for a couple of weeks, but I had already heard about a previous vicar, ostensibly the gentlest of men, who used to visit the little school at Rievaulx every Friday and administer a caning to the big boys – too big to be disciplined by the slight nuns who ran the school. Being caned by an ambassador for the One whose name is love sends slightly conflicting signals.

The Head whisked me away for an incredibly long chat about school stuff, and all the ways we could work together. We shared the same view of children, that they were the gift to be offered to the world's future, and that it was our job to enable every single child to flourish. We then toured the school. The Head of Music was doing composing with Year 9, and amazingly was harnessing them all as budding Beethovens. A history teacher was doing the Bayeux Tapestry, and was struggling with the Latin, so I helped him out – out of the corner of my eye I could see the Head scowling at him. A science teacher was demonstrating waves on a Cathode Ray Oscilloscope, or rather demonstrating a green straight line until I tweaked the knobs, adjusting the amplitude to produce a wave that would have done any surfer proud. 'I'm a biologist, not a physicist,' the teacher explained, good naturedly. 'I'm a physicist just doing this vicar's job until the right science post comes up!' I wasn't entirely joking.

The school seemed brilliant, keen to engage me across the curriculum, and I realised I was going to have great fun there. I often quipped when a baby cried during a service that its crying didn't bother me, since the wailing reminded me that the congregation might be alive, whereas otherwise I wasn't always so sure. This school clearly would keep my ministry alive when faced with so much deadness elsewhere. Some clergy style themselves as experts, taking faith into school; I style myself as a seeker, surprised and heartened by the faith and life I find in such places.

Friday, 26th September

Canons Garth originated as a twelfth-century medieval hall to house monks embarking on a spree of local church-building. It contains some curious ecclesiastical items. In the hall hangs a crucifix with a wooden figure of Jesus riddled with woodworm, making him look like the local rifle range had been using him for target practice. In the chapel (a handy thing to have in your home when you only have five other centres of worship in the parish!) there is another crucifix, where Jesus' arms are broken at his shoulders. Upstairs in one of the four attics we discovered a brass bedstead bearing no less than six mattresses, on top of which nestled a Madonna and child – the infant Jesus' foot was missing. Back in the chapel is another Madonna and child, this time Jesus is missing his hands, gazed at by the statue of a monk without a nose.

All these missing limbs in this strangest of houses puzzled me somewhat, until I chanced on a story about St Hugh of Lincoln, who roamed around in the same century as our new home was built. When visiting Fécamp Abbey his devotion to relics moved him to chew on Mary Magdalene's arm-bone while the guardians wailed, 'Oh, for shame!' In spite of their outraged protests, he bit off one of the saint's fingers, first with his front teeth and finally with his molars. Clearly on one of his pilgrimages he must have ended up in Helmsley and sated his appetite with Jesus' hands and feet, washed down with a monastic nose.

Eight hundred years on, Canons Garth seems a very tired building indeed, and I spend our first month there never more than a few feet away from my tool-box, involved in sundry repairs. This is frustrating since I want to be out and about as a parish priest but instead find myself stuck indoors being the curator/caretaker of the tattiest ancient monument. Another thing that disturbs me is that I have always set great store on honesty, but suddenly find myself the recipient of two lots of stolen goods: a fireplace in my study which was looted from the local castle in Victorian times, and tiling in the chapel which was nicked from nearby Rievaulx Abbey following its dissolution by Henry VIII in the 1530s.

While my family and I are watching a TV programme about the first atom bomb, a ceiling in the corridor collapses in sympathy, sending up a veritable mushroom cloud of wattle and daub last deployed in the Dark Ages; the mushroom cloud of dust blocking the struggling electric light means the Dark Ages have returned. Hasty repairs are completed followed by Helmsley's decorator, who has a striking doppelganger in that he is the spitting image of Lord Feversham, the local peer who appointed me to this pile. Lord Feversham is a practical sort, and like all true nobility dresses down, whereas the decorator dresses up and is quite a philosopher. In the understandable muddle, I fear I have instructed my Lord to apply a second coat to the newly repaired ceiling while bemusing the decorator with a lengthy treatise on the intricacies of the Church of England's Pastoral Measure.

🦋 Monday, 29th September

I decide to escape Canons Garth's clutches and visit one of my hamlet churches. A recent RSPCA advert about the gruelling physiological effects that stag-hunting has on the stag springs to mind. Heart pounding, glucose levels falling, fatty acid levels rising, red blood corpuscles rupturing: all four symptoms are there in abundance as I cycle to my moorland church up the 1:3 hill out of Helmsley. Four and a half gruelling miles later I reach the top of the moors, then freewheel down Cow House Bank, breathing in deep gulps of pine-saturated air, splashing through a ford before coming to rest on the opposite bank, leaning my bike against an ancient red telephone box, literally in the middle of nowhere. Hidden in nearby rhododendron bushes is a tiny Temple Moor church, celebrated by John Betjeman, no less, in his *Perp. Revival i' the North* (in a curious Scottish dialect) as he encountered it on a decidedly circuitous route, when he was 'gang tae' Harrogate. No one in their right mind would gang tae Harrogate via the forlorn and forsaken North York Moors, but I suppose poets have to be allowed their licence.

A century earlier, a posse of curates used to ride up here by horseback on Saturday night, sleep in a hammock slung across the south aisle, before tipping themselves out next morning before the altar, just in time to celebrate communion for the Earl and his 200 tenants who liberally peppered the hills. Now the curates are an extinct species, the farmers virtually so, but the little church and its school house remains, celebrated in the aforementioned verse by John Betjeman as:

> a stane kirk wi' a wee spire
> And a verra wee south aisle.

It was the first church designed by architect Temple Moore, with a characteristic painted wagon roof and stepped bell tower, which clearly caught Betjeman's imagination:

> For there's something in the painted roof
> And the mouldings round the door,
> The braw bench and the plain font
> That tells o' Temple Moore.

Nikolaus Pevsner raved about it as well as Betjeman, stating in his guide that 'the young architect obviously enjoyed this job thoroughly, and his pleasure is still infectious.' Sitting in this lovely little church getting my breath back after the long cycle ride, I could fully understand their enthusiasm, and could see myself making frequent pilgrimage here in the years that followed, in the spirit of no less than Christ, who kept stealing away from the hustle and bustle of ministry to recharge in quiet lonely places:

> The rhododendrons bloom wi'oot
> On ilka Simmer's day,
> And it's there the Airl o'Feversham
> Wad hae his tenants pray ...
> > 'Perp. Revival i' the North', High and Low (1966)

Vicars as well as tenants, I thought, as their prayers merged with mine.

I broke my return cycle-ride by popping into what seemed the most isolated farmhouse in Christendom – when St John ends his Gospel by talking about the good news of Jesus reaching the very ends of the earth, this was clearly the place he

had in mind. I sat in the stifling hot kitchen, an Aga dominating
one wall, belching out heat. My discussion with the ruddy-
faced farmer about peat-cutting and lambing took a surprisingly theological turn. 'You know, Vicar, we'd a reet good time
on our 'oliday in Turkey. We visited these old caves, in which
they'd carved out Christian churches. One of the churches had
been built BC, BC would you believe. You can't get much more
ancient than that!' My mind wandered for a moment as I
recalled a notice board I had spotted outside a church near
Bridlington which had proclaimed, a tad over-enthusiastically,
'Christian Worship has gone on at this spot for over two
thousand years.' Akin to the Irish Roman Catholic priest who
got more than a bit carried away in his homily, declaring that
when he was a boy, Jesus loved nothing better than going into
the synagogue and praying before the Blessed Sacrament. The
priest's surprised congregation had hardly recovered before his
further assertion that when she was a girl, the Blessed Virgin
Mary never failed to say the rosary every single day.

I realised the farmer had moved on from telling me about his
holiday in Turkey, and was regaling me with tales of East Moors,
surprisingly not untouched by the Second World War. 'We had
70 evacuees at the school, bombed out o' their homes in
Middlesbrough and Hull.' Although I had only glimpsed the
schoolhouse adjacent to the church, I tried to imagine how
they had managed to squeeze 70 kids into such a tiny place;
perhaps they'd slept standing up. The farmer continued, 'Poor
little buggers, they thought they'd got away from all the fireworks, but on their first day here, the RAF had used the moors
as target practice for their firebombs, and accidentally set fire to
the heather. That night the Luftwaffe flew over, aiming to bomb
t' steelworks by t' River Tees, but when they saw the fires on the
moor they mistook them for t' steel furnace ovens and dropped
their load over us. It were out of t' frying pan into t' fire for
those kids, out of t' frying pan into t' fire, a real fire an' all, if you

get my meaning!' he broke off, tears running down his face at this weakest of jokes. He fumbled in his mud-stained corduroy trousers for a handkerchief, but finding none snatched the tea towel hanging from the side of the Aga and dried his eyes with that. He then loudly blew his nose on it before replacing it on the rail.

'Another time we had an RAF pilot who'd bailed out of his stricken plane and ended up at Low Farm, dragging his parachute behind him. After giving him a glass or two to revive his spirits, they took him to t' phone box, you know, one by your church, and he rang his base in York asking them to come and pick him up. "Where are you?" they asked. "East Moors," he replied. "Where the hell's that?" He'd managed to get a map off the farmer so gave them the grid reference. "Bloody hell!" they said, "We can't spare anybody to come to that backwater until a week next Tuesday." Now in't that funny?' said the farmer, dabbing his eyes once again. 'T' RAF could fly to France or Germany in a couple of hours, but it took them o'er a week to get here to get one of their boys back! O'er a week, would you believe it! Why, you'd think this was the end of the world!' Tears of incredulity ran down his cheeks until he dabbed them with the tea towel, loudly blew his nose on it again before going over to the sink and using it to dry a couple of mugs. 'Now, Vicar, can I interest you in a cup o' tea?' he asked, as he picked up a jug of milk from the side, yellow stains of dried-up milk around the rim, and poured a little into the newly dried cups. I could smell the milk's sourness from the other side of the kitchen. But the first rule of visiting is never to decline hospitality, so I closed my eyes, drank my tea and thought of stags.

Fortunately the rancid tea had no immediate ill effects, so I whizzed down from the moors back to my new home. The view is absolutely stunning as you drop down into the town, the red roofs, the wounded castle, the proud church tower all presenting a panorama before your eyes. Despite the problems with the oldest vicarage in captivity and the challenge of trying to move on the oldest congregation in captivity, I feel so fortunate to be here. As the Queen said in Alan Bennett's play, *A Question of Attribution*, as she surveys the wonderful grounds of Buckingham Palace, 'I suppose heaven will be a bit of a come down after all this!' Perhaps Princess Diana will come back to reassure her.

Friday, 3rd October

I came to in the middle of a heated debate around the breakfast table about the relative importance of my wife's fortieth and my daughter's twelfth birthday. I plumped for twelve, the only age of Jesus recorded by the Gospels. My attempt to diffuse argument with theology was hijacked by an increasingly bizarre speculation about what form our Lord's twelfth birthday party took.

'Mum, can I have the twelve disciples, one for each year?'

'Well, let Judas win at musical chairs this time. He got so upset when he was first one out last year, especially after Lazarus' stunning performance in that game of Sleeping Lions. And don't spend all your time with Pete, Jimmy and Johnny and ignore the others. What about having a few girls for a change?'

'Good idea, Mum. How about Mary Mags, you know, the one with the red pigtails?'

'Er, OK, but she'll have to leave her seven devils at home. And another thing: don't upstage the conjurer this time; Nazareth's allotments have yet to recover from the 5000 rabbits you produced from his prayer shawl last year.'

'All right, Mum, but only if we can play hide and seek in Jerusalem at the Passover. And can we have fish sandwiches and red-wine jelly for tea? And what about a birthday cake in the shape of a cross again?'

The Passion seems so less angular, when played out by children happy in their parents' love.

🦋 Sunday, 5th October

Oldest congregation in captivity they might be (the combined age of the two churchwardens is over 150) but they couldn't have given us a more wonderful and friendly welcome, not least performing Herculean tasks to clean up Canons Garth. Yet all that being said, my first Sunday after being officially put in was more than a bit depressing. The cathedral-like parish church has the highest tradition, bells and smells and bowing and genuflections punctuating every paragraph. They had a little gong in the sanctuary which the server, the kindest and gentlest of men, took great pains to bong when I said our Lord's words over the bread and the wine. But the server didn't seem to notice that there was hardly anyone there in the congregation to appreciate his painstaking efforts. And if he did notice, it didn't seem to worry him, almost as if people were irrelevant as long as the job was done (which he was doing with great panache) and the high church fineries were observed. My great friend, Canon John Young, York Diocese's Missioner and Evangelist, had once quipped that the Church of England could be the first organisation in history to die because of an obsession with good taste.

Not that everything the service contained seemed that good to taste, more a mishmash of traditions and peculiarities foisted on the parish by previous vicars. I recalled the Bishop of Gloucester's tale about a high church where he worked as a newly ordained curate. On his first Sunday he was anxious to get all the ceremonial right, but something puzzled him. As the head server walked from one end of the sanctuary to the other, he bowed at the altar (nothing unusual in that) but a few steps later he brought his right knee almost up to his chin. When he came back across the sanctuary, he did exactly the same mannerism in the same place. 'What was all that about?' the embryonic bishop asked him after the service. 'Oh, there used to be a tall kneeler there!' the head server explained, as if the reason were obvious.

I suppose my first job at Helmsley is to be a bit of an Inspector Morse, and detect what used to be there, laying some ghosts, honouring others. The church building itself was quite a clue, in that a guy called Charles Gray who had been vicar for 43 years in the latter part of Queen Victoria's reign had set his stamp on the interior. Like Michaelangelo on LSD, he had daubed the north wall with paintings setting out the story of Christianity on a global and local canvas, imagining the Christian faith growing like a tree with fruits emerging like the Diocese of York, the parish of Helmsley, Rievaulx's Cistercian Abbey and (curiously) Lord Feversham and Canons Garth. The message was clear: God became man to bring Christianity to Helmsley. In a sense he did, the Holy Spirit indeed has a local accent, but primarily calls us to look at God at work on a wider canvas, humbly seeing every person in the world as his child. There was no humility in that wall, only self-promotion and self-importance, and it grated on me.

Gray daubed another wall in one of the cluttered transepts with a vivid depiction of good triumphing over evil. Good was represented by an anaemic white knight on a horse impaling a thirty-foot fire-breathing red dragon with his spear. Attached to the dragon were all the names of the Saxon and Viking Norse gods, which had been defeated as Christianity emerged as England's true faith. Just to press the point home, beneath the dragon was a picture of King Oswald and Bishop Aidan, northern saints from the seventh century, preaching to the good inhabitants of Helmsley and pressing home Christianity's cause. To be honest, it was the rather gorgeous dragon which drew my sympathy. As I looked from the impaled dragon to the impaled Christ on the massive crucifix on the altar below, I sensed the two had rather a lot in common. After all, both had been crucified by those who prefer the call to be ultra-orthodox, rather than heed the desire that the God whose name is love has for them.

Gray had brought the crucifix back from a trip to Oberammergau in an age when they were clearly less fussy about excess baggage. Gray also carried a heck of a lot of baggage from his ultra-orthodox father, Robert. As Archbishop of Cape Town, he had suspended his assistant bishop, Colenso, for doubting that the first five books of the Bible were pure history, as well as for being over-kind to much-married natives – Colenso allowed them to keep on their wives following their conversion to Christianity, rather than abandon them to certain destitution. Gray had then twisted the arm of the Archbishop of Canterbury to initiate a conference for Anglican bishops across the globe enforcing a fierce orthodoxy: thus was born the decadal Lambeth Conference, bane of every Archbishop's life ever since.

Archbishop Gray's son manifested all the fruits of his despotic father's spirit, including haranguing the local earl for his bad drains, insulting the saintly Abbot of Ampleforth by insisting on addressing him as plain 'Mr', deriding the local Roman Catholic Chapel as the 'Italian Mission', thrashing local pugilists with one hand tied behind his back, thrashing local children with both hands if he detected any whiff of disrespect, and even producing a magazine where he encouraged the ladies of the parish to avoid the perils of too tight corsetry with sentiments such as 'A woman is worth nothing if she cannot keep her house clean.'

Despite the myriad of scary stories I had unearthed about Gray, there were the occasional flashes of humour. In 1906 Gray had erected a massive black marble altar in memory of his late father in the transept, without any permission whatsoever from the diocesan authorities. The Archdeacon of Cleveland, ordered him to remove it. Gray's reply was terse: 'Archdeacon, I spent six yoke of oxen hauling that marble up from the railway station. If you wish to remove it, you can provide the oxen!' Ninety years on, I sensed that I was those oxen, sent not so much to remove all the illegal furnishings that my predecessor had imposed on the place, but rather to exorcise his spirit and free things up. Too many people are terrified of a God, fiercely made in Gray's image, who sits on a terrible throne of judgement; they need recalling to the God of our Lord Jesus Christ, whose name is love, and who sits on a mercy seat.

🍃 *Friday, 10th October*

Charles Gray, ever ambitious, planned to restore and re-roof the ruined Cistercian Abbey at Rievaulx, but was thwarted by too high costs, amounting to an exorbitant £30,000, a small fortune in Victorian times. Yet in recent times his aim to revive a powerhouse of prayer has been more modestly achieved, in that at the Abbey's west end lies a retreat house staffed by two nuns, whose quiet ministry bestows on the place a numinous sense of calm. Celebrating communion in their chapel is a sheer joy, although not without some surprises. 'David, will you change the reserved sacrament please?' the sister greeted me with on my first visit, as I arrived breathless after a gruelling pull on my cycle up from Helmsley.

'I'll be glad to, but where's the aumbry?' I replied, as I looked around the little chapel trying to detect the special cupboard in which the reserved sacrament is kept.

'Oh, it's in the dove,' she patiently explained, since I was clearly slow on the uptake with fine ecclesiastical detail. 'Its middle is hollowed out and contains a silver pyx.'

The metal dove dominated the little room, hovering over the altar, representing the Holy Paraclete, the Order with its Mother House at Whitby to which the nuns belonged. The Holy Paraclete is an alternative phrase for Holy Spirit, often symbolised as a dove. Letting the dove contain the bread consecrated at the Eucharist, which itself represented Jesus' body, struck me as forcing too many illusions into one metal bird. The said bird was suspended on a pulley system, which I had to lower towards the end of the communion service, so I could get the old bread out and put the new bread in. The dove, obviously in revenge for me being scathing about her multiple role, proved both mischievous and elusive. She swooped and nearly upset the chalice, before doing a sudden lurch and bashing me on the forehead. Having the Holy Paraclete come down at the Lord's Supper can obviously make for a disturbing time.

The dove wasn't the only disturbance; the effect of surface-tension also reared its ugly head. At the offertory I had prepared for communion and poured water and wine into the chalice. Unbeknown to me a drip of water had run down the flagon to its base, thereby sticking it to the glass tray on which it was standing (alongside the flask of wine) with the strength of superglue. At the ablutions following communion, I was distracted as I rubbed my sore forehead following the dove's assault. In a dazed state, as I innocently picked up the aforementioned flagon, the whole tray rose as well, catapulting the flask of wine across the carpeted chapel.

I was transformed in an instant from being a reverend father to being a dad, used to mopping up sundry spills. 'Have you got any kitchen paper?' I asked sister, in a novel form of post-communion greeting. She gave me a queer look – first I'd nutted their holy dove, and then I'd started sprinkling red wine all over the place. 'Don't worry, Vicar, I'll clear it up later,' she reassured me, obviously deciding that the best policy was to get me off the premises as soon as possible, before I caused further damage. But I insisted on getting on with the job, and used several sheets of kitchen roll to soak up the red wine before the stain set in. After our frantic post-Eucharistic ministrations the carpet looked as good as new.

When I trained for the ordained ministry, we were told that if you ever spilt consecrated wine on a sanctuary carpet or stone, you should summon a team of nuns who would devotedly lick the stones clean or even consume the carpet. Apparently this special top-secret order continuously travelled up and down the A1 in a Mini, and could be contacted by radio. I fancied shy Rievaulx might be the head office of this legendary itinerant order, which is why I acted so resolutely. I thought I had given the sisters enough trouble for one day, without adding indigestion caused by a surfeit of Axminster!

🍂 Sunday, 12th October

I was determined to inject the life I had found at the school into my new church, so for my second Sunday I conscripted my three daughters as servers. I appointed Clare, almost eight, to be a boat girl, not an exile braving the Indo-Chinese seas in a craft singularly unfitted for the purpose, but a robed child who carried a boat-shaped incense-bearing container for use at various points of the service when you wanted to asphyxiate the congregation with clouds of incense. Her sister, Hannah, two years her senior, was to carry the altar book and hold it for me to read the Gospel. Ruth was crucifer, taking her cue from Jesus who said that if anyone wanted to be his disciple, they should take up their cross and follow him. Ruth took up her cross and all the robed flunkies followed her.

The three girls took to their roles like ducks to water, and it was good to have their slightly mischievous company in the sanctuary. Before my time, women, even the vicar's wife, were forbidden to enter the sanctuary at Helmsley, which was a fiercely guarded male preserve, so it was no surprise that after the service someone took Rachel, my wife, aside and complained that the new servers should be boys and not girls. 'I'm so sorry,' my wife replied, with a mischievous glint in her eye. 'If only I'd known, I would have given birth to sons and not daughters!'

I recalled an apocryphal story about my former boss, Archbishop David Hope. Earlier in his career he had become vicar of one of the highest churches in the land. On his first Sunday, during Mass, he was heartily singing the offertory hymn while preparing the bread and wine on the altar. A head server sidled up to him with a face that looked like he was sucking on a lemon and snapped, 'Father, in this church we don't normally sing in the sanctuary.'

'I'm the vicar, it's my church, it's my sanctuary and if I want to sing in the sanctuary, I'll bloody well sing in the sanctuary. You just mind your own business,' David Hope replied, treating him to the full force of his Yorkshire bluntness.

My other boss as Archbishop of York's chaplain was John Habgood, and oddly enough as I unpacked my books following our move, a page fell open that he had written in 1962: 'The Church is a horrible human institution, and the only justification for it is that occasionally God shines through, and beyond the ghastly clothes and the rest of it, one discovers a love that surprises one.'

Just before moving to Helmsley, I had been reading a brilliant book called *Candle in the Darkness* by Patrick Thomas, which explored the priorities set by Christian disciples in Wales. He quotes from a play about the life of a seventeenth-century Welsh mystic, Morgan Lloyd, where the playwright charts his hero's progress through the veritable roller-coaster of religious controversies of that age. Not surprisingly, by the end of the play Lloyd has reached a state of total disillusionment and despair. He pours out his agony in a desperate plea to God, 'O God, come, come, bring your holy death to kiss me to your own clear, shining light.' There is complete silence, and then Lloyd's little son comes on to the stage. He calls to his father quietly and affectionately and Lloyd looks at him, as though hearing a voice for the first time. He stretches out his hand to the boy, who takes it. Then his small daughter comes in and calls to him, and he offers her his other hand. Morgan's wife then joins them, carrying their baby. She gives the child to her husband, and cradling the little one in his arms, he begins to sing her a nursery rhyme. The others join in. The play's author, John Gwilym Jones, tells us that the play should end on 'a note of quiet, affectionate joy'. The playwright's message is that God will not be found in obsession with ceremony, or in abstruse and bitter theological and political wrangling. He will, however, be found in the loving kindness that is present in close human relationships at their best. When his son calls him, Lloyd recognises the voice of love which is the very voice of God. He sees that the things which he had thought significant, the agonising soul-searching, the anguished spiritual quest and all the complex doctrinal confrontations, were really irrelevant. God was not present in them, but was present in the little family whom Lloyd had neglected and ignored for so long.

And so say all of us! Having my little family surround me in the sanctuary wasn't just to keep me company, but was making a major theological point.

Monday, 13th October

While my new parish skirts the southern edge of the moors, the neighbouring parish takes the peaks and the troughs of the moors full on, with villages perched on the highest hill tops over one thousand feet above sea level. On the map one village looks as if it's just a stone's throw from another, but in reality one village will be on the top of one hill, the other village on top of another, with miles of road ribboning up and down the valleys connecting them. The neighbouring parish has a new vicar too, so I drive over to his institution for a quaint little ceremony where the bishop puts in a new parish priest, while at the same time encouraging the parish not to be put out by a new broom sweeping them clean. The route to the church where it is all going to happen is a strange one. I expected to be motoring up hill and down dale, but what was marked as a ford turned out to be a drive for a quarter of a mile along a rough river bed. The recent wet spell caused a veritable torrent to foam darkly around my wheel arches, and there were several moments when I feared the fierce current was going to force my car in a direction neither the engine nor the steering wished it to go. While David crossing the River Rye didn't carry quite the kudos of Moses crossing the Red Sea or Joshua crossing the River Jordan, I felt a definite sense of deliverance when the road opted to end its dalliance with the river and rose up the wooded hillside towards the church.

I obviously wasn't the only one, in that most of the faces in the little moorland church sported the relieved look of a Jonah spewed out from the waves. A rotund organist, perched at the front, several sizes too large for the little harmonium he was attempting to play, struck up the first hymn, 'Jerusalem'. 'Bring me my arrows of desire,' sang the distinctly unerotic congregation, cocooned in the heaviest overcoats which would have masked the charms of even an Adonis or Venus. The organist got a bit carried away with Parry's masterpiece, pumping furiously at the bellows, feet pedalling faster than a mountain-biker ascending Snowdon, making the harmonium rock dangerously. During the hymn the beaming bishop was led down the narrowest of aisles by no less than ten churchwardens (two for each church in the parish), all ruddy-faced farmers squeezed into their Sunday best, looking like Sumos in suits.

Hymn over, the vicar was taken on a tour of the church, pausing at the font, main door and altar, like a new dog marking his territory, before finally ringing the church bell to show he had truly taken possession. He proved a bit over-enthusiastic as a campanologist, giving the bell-rope such a tug that a bit of plaster from the tower ceiling clattered down, turning his hair white in an instant. Or maybe it turned white because of the sheer terror of ministry that awaited him. The Archdeacon then led him by the hand (enter gay weddings again) to his stall from where he gave the notices, the usual thing, next Sunday's round of services, sundry harvest festivals and suppers, before a strange little declaration that his wife (also ordained) was a far better priest than him. The heavily overcoated, and by now over-heated and distinctly fragrant congregation, looked unmoved; ever since the Reformation in these parts, without question they have rated Mrs Vicar as the superior pastor.

Following the service we adjourned to the village hall for a bunfight which from the look of it had been prepared several hours before. The ham sandwiches were curling at the edges, the sausage rolls had that pasty look, the sponge cakes had sunk, and the humid day had given several meat-flies a new lease of life, enabling them to sample the feast before us. I recall a bishop whispering *sotto voce* to his chaplain, faced by a similar repast on a very hot summer's day, 'What a wonderful spread, a million flies can't be wrong!' I just had a cup of tea.

🔖 *Sunday, 19th October*

To cheer up proceedings following our main service, we've introduced a couple of things. Rachel has started running a

Traidcraft stall in the porch, so that those leaving church, having prayed for the world's poor, can actually do something positive about it. Secondly we've started serving refreshments. Not everyone likes this, in that they feel strongly that the church building should be a sacred place rather than a place of fellow-ship and hospitality, 'My temple should be a house of prayer, you have made it a coffee shop,' sort of line. One stalwart got more than a bit carried away, hectoring me as she pointed her bony finger threateningly towards me, 'You start serving tea and coffee after church, Vicar, and you'll be marrying homosexuals next!'

As it happens, I'm not that great a fan of after-service tea and coffee myself, but I felt we ought to do something to defrost things and other people liked the idea. The Maker of the stars and sea visiting us in bread and wine strikes me as demanding a hushed awe, instead of a forced conversation about someone's magnificent hydrangea bloom, or marvelling over a genius of a grandson who has scraped a Grade E in Design and Technology. As Kierkegaard quipped, 'God did not become man to make small talk.' Even so, I realise my view might have something to do with my basic shyness, and I also concede that often small talk can lead to big talk.

This morning my youngest daughter, Clare, cheered the proceedings by introducing her new pet hamster to the assem-bly. Quite desperate for any topic of conversation, they all swooped upon the rodent, who promptly retaliated by biting the nearest finger, that of one of the sweetest of nuns from Rievaulx. Her having an impressive set of stigmata imposed on her by the vicar's daughter's pet opened the floodgates for a tidal wave of medical care, with sundry dressings hastily constructed out of kitchen paper and tea towels, with anxious checks about rabies.

The whole episode was a bit of a nightmare, and resulted in my having a nightmare. I am due to lead the Advent Retreat at the nuns' mother house at Sneaton Castle in Whitby, and in my dream I foolishly took the hamster with me. Not a single nun turned up for my addresses. Like a creature from a Saki short story (I had recently read *Sredni Vashtar*), the hamster, with her newly acquired taste for nuns' blood, had run amok and had massacred the whole mother house.

With heart thumping, I gratefully awoke from my dream, yearning for safe conversations about hydrangeas and infant prodigies, and even marrying homosexuals.

Sunday, 26th October

At the end of a busy morning, I cycle up to Sproxton, a church serving a village perched on the top of the hill, with spectacular views over the vales to the north and south. This is my third visit to the church (one harvest festival and two bog-standard Sundays) and each time I have found the small congregation remarkably cheerful, a hill-top people with a hill-top, upbeat mentality, rather than a dour, depressed valley mentality. On a Sunday I preach to them the same sermon that I preached at Helmsley, but find that jokes and humorous anecdotes that have fallen flat at Helmsley have them rolling in the aisles at Sproxton, or rolling in the aisle, since it is the tiniest of ancient churches.

The altar book is ancient too, pages yellowing with a musty smell, spanning the decades. The prayer for the monarch has Victoria crossed out and replaced with Edward, who then too is crossed out and replaced with George. Edward is briefly reinstated, but then angrily smudged out even before the ink is dry. George is then reinstated for a more respectable period before he too deferred to Elizabeth, squeezed into an already overcrowded margin. There is no room for a new monarch: it will either have to be a new book or a new constitution.

Actually I left the altar book untouched, using a more modern order of service which I had printed off. The dozen-strong congregation shared the Peace gladly rather than reluctantly, and my comment about how many handshakes would be involved if everyone shook hands with everyone else there resulted in a four-page note being delivered to Canons Garth later in the day. One of the members of the congregation had been a Maths teacher, and my aside had caused her to revisit arithmetic and geometric and binomial series galore. It's not the first time that mathematical thoughts have been sparked off during a church service. Galileo Galilei, bored at a Mass in Pisa Cathedral in the sixteenth century, watched a swinging incense burner which was suspended from the roof, and noticed however wide it swung it still took the same time. He even worked out a formula for the period of swing, namely $T = 2\pi\sqrt{\frac{l}{g}}$, indicating that it must have been a very long sermon indeed.

Wednesday, 29th October

Not a lot of people know this (shades of Michael Caine) but if you can't get to church, the church can come to you. People *in extremis*, too ill or infirm to get out, can have communion brought to them, so that they can focus without distraction on supping with their Saviour at the twilight of their lives. Or at least that's the theory. In practice many aren't that infirm, but it's simply more convenient to have communion delivered rather than trouble to go to church. As a curate in Middlesbrough, I once took communion to one old lady, only, later that lunchtime, to find her ahead of me in the fish and chip shop queue, looking more than a bit sheepish.

Those who are genuinely housebound, who in theory have got all the time in the world for your visit, have the fullest timetable of callers who vie for your space. I'm relaxed about competing with nurses and doctors, in that we are all busy people, promoting physical and spiritual health. I'm less happy about being kicked into touch by hairdressers and manicurists, and am most irked by the omnipresent Ringtons Tea man, who invariably will boldly interrupt my word of life with his merry take on the benefits of Earl Grey tea or garibaldi biscuits. But more than occasionally, God shines through and surprises you with the most lowly and holy of lives.

Such as today. I tapped on the window and patiently waited, the torrential rain pouring on my uncovered head, beads of water gathering on my woollen cloak. Eventually the door was opened, just the tiniest crack. 'Who is it?' 'It's David, Sister Lillian, the new vicar. I've come to bring you communion.'

She opened the door a few inches wider, and I squeezed through, walking into a set as medieval as Hannah Hauxwell's farm in the upper Dales, featured on *Too Long a Winter*. Except that Sister Lillian, unlike Hannah, didn't even have a pair of cows to keep her warm. Just a dog, which moulted more hair than the rest of the hounds of the parish put together. He continually orbited my legs during the service, like a sheepdog rounding up his solitary flock, condemning my cassock and cloak to be trimmed with dog-fur for the rest of the week.

Sister Lillian was breathless after admitting me, a high price to pay for making her communion. We couldn't start the service before she had had her 'beer', a sip of Dandelion and Burdock which I decanted into a drinking bottle for her, the viscous liquid bubbling over and making my hands sticky.

In the pocket of her painfully worn cardigan was an individual apple pie, which she removed and put on the sofa arm. 'If I lie down, I might squash it,' she explained. Then from the very same pocket she produced some scraps of raw meat, which she pressed into my hands to feed the dog. 'Is there much sickness in the parish?' she asked, with genuine concern. 'There will be,' I thought, 'if we keep carrying on like this.' I stole into the kitchen to wash my hands, only to be appalled that it was so primitive. One cold tap above a chipped Belfast sink, a battered cabinet or two, piled high with chipped unwashed crockery, food dried on it from goodness knows when. On one plate there was even a discoloured bit of Spam; there was me, thinking Spam had been eradicated along with smallpox!

I rinsed my hands under the tap, and shook them clean rather than dry them on the grubby towel that was draped over a chair. I returned to Lillian, who was suffering from an attack of burping, no doubt caused by the Dandelion and Burdock. Not wanting to embarrass her, I averted my eyes, instead scanning the severely cluttered room. On the dampest of walls, festooned with pictures in damaged frames, hung an MBE. 'Goodness, Lillian, is that yours?' I asked in surprise. 'Oh yes, Vicar, King George VI presented it to me, for nothing really. All I'd done was to run a Church Army refreshment caravan for the troops in the last war.'

I realised the immensity of all she had done, as she told me how she had hawked her caravan all over Britain and Europe, chasing the action. Lillian was there to cheer the troops who were dragging bodies of their comrades out of the English Channel, following some doomed rehearsal for D-Day, right through to the relief of Belsen, which proved the most harrowing sights of all, the emaciated victims too late to be cheered by Lillian's tea and buns. I began to understand a little bit why, having witnessed such deprivation and desolation, possessions and home comforts meant nothing to her. 'I feel so sorry for all those victims of such a terrible war,' I commented, ineptly.

'My family were war victims,' Sister Lillian boldly declared, as if that qualified her to have a solidarity with all victims. 'Our house in Sunderland was shelled just before Christmas 1914, when those German destroyers strafed the North East's resorts.

Then the Luftwaffe bombed us again in 1940. My auntie was gassed, too,' she told me, a surprisingly proud ring to her tones.

'Gassed?' I exclaimed. 'I didn't think the UK mainland was subject to gas attacks.'

'Well, the bomb that hit our house in 1940 made a massive crater by our front door. My auntie, in a panic, ran out of the house and fell straight into it and knocked herself out. At the bottom of the hole was a ruptured gas pipe, which gassed her as she lay there. The ARPs found her and carried her on a stretcher to Sunderland hospital. She came round after a day or two, though, and was none the worse for wear. Well, not too much worse.'

She suddenly changed tack and asked me what I was reading, a tender concern, one minister checking up on another, anxious that I was being spiritually fed. 'Oh, I'm reading a book about John the Baptist,' I replied.

'Ooh, John the Baptist, John the Baptist, now he was a very good man, a very good man', she explained, as if he was a personal acquaintance. 'Mind you,' she added after a moment's thought, 'not as good as Jesus!' as if the two lads had helped staff her army canteen and been weighed up by her shrewd gaze.

I gave her communion and then held her hand as I gave her my blessing. Or did she give a blessing to me?

Sunday, 9th November

When he interviewed me for the post, Lord Feversham had made it very clear that for him and all his merry men, Remembrance Sunday was the high point of the Christian year. My first ever Remembrance Sunday as a clergyman, way back in 1981, had not gone well. I was helping out at a very plush parish near Middlesbrough, and boldly preached to the startled congregation that people had not died in two world wars for three million to be unemployed at Mrs Thatcher's whim, nor had they died for us to live under the threat of nuclear holocaust. Every one had shaken my hand at the door and said, 'Nice sermon, Vicar,' but then twenty of them went on to complain to the Bishop of Whitby about this troublesome priest. I was hauled before him and had to explain myself. Before the interview I sent him all the sermons I had ever preached, and actually we had a good discussion, despite him being a high Tory and me being a Bennite. But I learned my lesson and realised that folk can be a tad sensitive around 11th November.

Remembrance Sunday in Helmsley has a nice twist, in that the actor Ian Carmichael takes a major lead, having served in a regiment stationed here in the Second World War. So in the week before Remembrance Sunday, Ian Carmichael popped down from his home near Whitby and met up with me in the church to pace out the service and check everything was in order. Our visit coincided with a coach trip from Liverpool, who were seeking shelter in the church, searching for mice – oak ones, the trademark of Thompsons of Kilburn, the local carpenters. Eventually one elderly Liverbird, abandoning her quest for mice, interrupted our plotting. 'Excuse me, I hope you don't mind uz askin', but are you Ian Carmichael, luv?'

'I am indeed,' Ian Carmichael replied, Lord Peter Wimsey to a tee.

'I'm proud to meet you; you've given uz such pleasure,' said the lady, shaking him warmly by the hand. Service preparations had to be abandoned as a queue of communion-length proportions developed down the church, all eager to shake the hand of the man himself. Ian Carmichael gallantly brushed the drops of rain off the shoulders of one admirer. 'We don't want you catching your death,' he explained, no doubt rehearsing for his forthcoming role as director of the hospital in ITV's Sunday night series, *The Royal*.

Ian Carmichael was attached to the 22nd Dragoons, a flail tank regiment, who were stationed here in Duncombe Park, Lord Feversham's estate, for two years' training from 1942 to 1944. Their operational role on D-Day, verging on the suicidal, was to clear a path through minefields so that assault forces behind them could pass through and attack heavily defended enemy positions. Given their role bridging land and sea, the tradition at Helmsley is to always sing 'Eternal Father, strong to save, whose arm doth bind the restless wave,' on Remembrance Sunday. It is a sobering fact that in the time it took us to sing the hymn, the regiment had already lost a dozen of their comrades, with scores more wounded.

Half a dozen surviving members of the regiment joined us and paraded their standard, while Ian Carmichael read Jesus' words from John's Gospel, 'Greater love have no man than this, that he lays down his life for his friends.' The other lesson was read by a young man just turned 18; the poignancy of the occasion doubled as it dawned on the congregation that back in 1944 he would have been fighting for his life and ours on Normandy's far-away beaches.

Poignant moments aside, the Dragoons' preparations for D-Day, with which Ian Carmichael had regaled me, struck me as more *Dad's Army* than *Band of Brothers*. Most of their time around here was filled with dealing with moorland fires: tedious, repetitive, smoky work, beating out burning heather which re-ignited the instant your back was turned. After one such weary day, Ian Carmichael was enjoying a well-earned dinner in the Officers' Mess at Duncombe Park, perched on a hill above Helmsley. He was taken aside by the colonel. 'Did you and your men manage to put out all the fires on the moors?' the colonel barked. 'Er, yes, sir,' Ian Carmichael stuttered. 'Then would you mind stepping outside with me for a moment?' the colonel ordered. Ian Carmichael followed his commanding officer and both men gazed at the night sky, the horizon ablaze in every direction. I suppose it's the same with winning a war: you think you've brought peace once and for all, but turn your back for an instant and strife flares up once again.

🪶 *Thursday, 20th November*

Her name is Laura. Although she has Down's Syndrome, her parents had opted to have her educated mainstream at our local primary school. It was tonight as I attended the school's production of *Joseph and the Amazing Technicolor Dreamcoat* in the local Arts Theatre that I first noticed her. The temperature of the tiny Arts Theatre was tropical, in stark contrast to the chilly November fog which had been hanging around for days. I was there as a proud parent of Hannah (an angel) and Clare (a servant). Laura was a dancer, fawning upon Pharaoh as he performed a pastiche of Elvis Presley, as Pharaohs were wont to do when they took a welcome break from their extensive programme of pyramid and sphinx building. Laura got more than carried away with her Showaddywaddy dance and all eyes in the theatre were on her rather than a by now distinctly piqued Pharaoh. My knowledge of ancient history was patchy, but I seemed to recall that it's best to avoid piquing Pharaohs.

The audience laughed, at first gales of laughter of the liberal tolerant sort, 'What a card this Down's Syndrome child is!' But then the mood changed to one of utter amazement, that any child was capable of giving herself so utterly, in such a lock, stock and barrel way. Here was no less than a latter-day David, King David who had danced with joy before the Lord when his army had finally taken Jerusalem, even doing cartwheels before his band of adoring maidens, doubly excited because underwear had yet to be invented. His wife, Michal (perhaps understandably) despised him for putting his heart and soul, mind and strength into his gyrations. No one in our audience despised Laura; quite the contrary, the theatre was as one, everyone deeply moved.

I heard today about another entry as dramatic as Laura's, but for different reasons. A governor at Ryedale School and part-time firefighter (affectionately known as Nee-Naw-Nicky) was billed to talk to a Year 7 class on fire prevention. She thought she would make a surprising start by kicking the door open and then crawling into the classroom on her belly, pretending it was smoke-filled. To complete the charade, she decked herself out in uniform complete with breathing apparatus, including a mask and an oxygen tank strapped to her back, wielding a fireman's axe in her hand. The only problem with her absolutely brilliant idea was that the mask fogged up a bit and she got the wrong classroom. Which meant that Year 10, Set 1, who should have been immersed in the heady poetry of *Romeo and Juliet* were, to say the least, startled by this axe-wielding firewoman writhing through the entire length of their classroom. Once they had recovered, the brighter ones even suggested amending the text:

'But soft, what light through yonder window breaks? It might be a fire – call Nee-Naw-Nicky!'

Shakespeare eat your heart out …

My wife, having unpacked myriad boxes, and despaired of ever shaping Canons Garth into the modern residence she has always desired, has been doing a bit of supply teaching at Ryedale. It's demanding work, but Rachel is constantly cheered by incidents such as Nee-Naw-Nicky's, as well as the innocent mistakes that children make. Someone in her Year 11 RE Group, when asked in an Ethics test to define promiscuity, wrote: 'Promiscuity is the weirdest sensation that somehow you've been somewhere before.' She went on to invigilate a Year 10 Food Technology test which asked for an example of a dish whose preparation didn't require pre-heating the oven. One pupil's answer: coleslaw!

All her classes seem intrigued by the fact that she is married to a vicar. The Year 10, Set 4 English Group are, to say the least, a challenge and constantly plague her with irrelevant questions, such as 'Miss, does your husband actually receive money for being a vicar?' There was an incredulity in the child's voice which suggested I ought to be charged rather than paid for inflicting holiness on my flock.

'Er, yes, of course he gets paid,' my wife replied.

'How much, Miss? Fifty thousand pounds a year?'

'Nah, don't be daft,' a loutish lad loudly interrupted. 'If he was paid as much as that, do you think she'd be here teaching us lot?' I warmed to him; I've always felt that people who truly realise how awful they are are not far from the kingdom of heaven.

I relayed the episode to our archdeacon's wife who is a retired teacher. She told me how the worldly wise 16-year-old girls in her form eventually rumbled the fact that she was a vicar's wife. 'Are you really married to a clergyman, Miss?' they asked incredulously.

'Yes I am,' she admitted.

'But you won't have any children, though,' the gals pressed.

'Well, yes, we've got four actually.'

'Eeh, Miss,' they replied, looking utterly shocked. 'How could you, how could you, Miss, with a vicar?!' I blush to repeat how the dishy archdeacon's wife responded to them.

◗ Sunday, 23rd November

I've got to that time of life when I really do need reading glasses. For instance, last night my myopic eye chanced on this in the lonely hearts column of our local rag: 'Single nun seeks energetic male for fun outings and more.' For a full two minutes I poured forth a tirade on the lax standards within our religious communities, until my daughters checked the column and banished my pitiful apoplexy, 'Dad, the word is mum, not nun!'

I was still having trouble this morning at the early Communion, when the Gospel was about Jesus healing the multi-possessed Legion. Instead of reading, 'He cast the devils into a herd of swine,' I pronounced, 'He cast the disciples into a herd of swine.' I quickly corrected myself, but then spent the rest of the service musing that our frustrated Lord must have been sorely and repeatedly tempted to carry out my mis-read.

Perhaps it's nothing to do with needing glasses at all. As a young, clear-eyed curate I developed the knack of silently reading the next line of a Bible passage in my head before blurting it out loud. I was reading the Gospel where Jesus makes the long trawl to heal Jairus' daughter. Jesus and shy young me had just successfully navigated the woman with long-term gynae problems, when alarm bells rang in my head as I saw this line coming up: 'Someone came from Jairus' house and said, "Your daughter is dead. Trouble the rabbit no further." '

'What rabbit? Where on earth has that crept in?' I thought, panic rising, until I mercifully realised that I was seeing a *t* which simply wasn't there. But I've often wondered since, had I actually said the word out loud, how I would have extricated myself. Here followeth the Gospel according to Animal Hospital:

'What rabbit?' Jesus said.

'Oh, it's my daughter's pet,' Jairus replied. 'She doted on him. He'll be wracked with grief if he realises she is dead. We'll have to do our best to keep it from him ...'

I wonder if I would have got away with it. After all, I was the mischievous curate who added the fictitious neonlites and nylontites to the tedious list of tribes outlined in Joshua 3:10; and not a member of the Evensong congregation batted an eyelid.

Oddly enough, an inversion of that rabbit story happened at Bishopthorpe Palace. Before the entrance to the archiepiscopal offices is a gate in the outside wall, which divides the river terraces from the rest of the grounds. 'Please keep this gate shut – it keeps the rabbits out,' a notice read. 'Why do you need to keep the rabbis out?' a visiting bishop anxiously asked me. Good question. As a life-long fan of Rabbi Lionel Blue, I firmly believe that welcoming the rabbis rather than excluding them can only enrich and cheer our faith. And as Rowan Williams said, 'When we build a safe stockade around ourselves and our like-believing friends, we should beware that at the other side of our self-imposed wall stands Christ, gently waving at us.' Christ, a rabbi amongst rabbis.

🍃 Sunday, 30th November

The ancient notebook, bound in dusty leather, written in longhand, had lain hidden in a paper carrier bag in our attic along with the six mattresses and sundry damaged statues for aeons. Until just before Advent 1997, when I opened its pages, the hairs bristle on the back of my neck …

It all started innocently enough with a letter campaign in the *Church Times* (that Anglican ecclesiastical comic) about anti-Judaic tendencies lurking in 'Lo he comes with clouds descending'. The hymn looms here somewhat, set as it is to the tune, HELMSLEY. In my first few months I have received earnest enquiries about the connection, and as Advent looms lost friends have made contact, flattering me that singing 'Lo he comes …' would remind them of my existence.

Investigation of the deep wailing at the true Messiah in the hymn's second verse, so offensive to modern-day Jews, revealed an allusion to Revelation 1:7, itself highly dependent on Mat-

thew 24:30 and Luke 23:27 and 48. I recalled my time in the
Council of Christians and Jews, how so often we came to the
Catch 22 conclusion: if only we could scrap the New Testament,
we Christians and Jews would get on famously.

However unpalatable the deep wailing of those who pierced
and nailed him to the tree might be, the original was far worse.
Moravian minister John Cennick's 1752 version was quickly
honed by Charles Wesley, who wisely omitted excesses, including 'Countless trumpets blow before his bloody sign', and
'Welcome, welcome, bleeding Lamb!' You can't have drunken
chants from the Banquet of the Guild of Butchers infecting
respectable hymnody.

As the words mutated, so did the tune, first appearing in
1765 in Wesley's *Select Hymns with Tunes Annext*, named OLIV-
ERS after its composer. By 1769 a similar tune, published by
Martin Madan, is called HELMSLEY. In the intervening years,
a certain Richard Conyers, Vicar of Helmsley, had published *A
Collection of Psalms and Hymns, from various authors: for the use of
serious and devout Christians of every denomination*, and it may well
be that Conyers, inebriated by his hymnbook's snazzy title,
forced the name change. 'Just a minute,' I thought, as the name
Conyers rang bells. 'Didn't I come across his handwritten
memoirs when we were clearing out the attics?'

I poured over the arachnid handwriting and discovered a
local boy made good, tediously good (to coin Saki's phrase),
loved by everyone, high and low. None other than *How-sweet-
the-name-of-Jesus-sounds* John Newton described him as perhaps
the most exemplary, indefatigable and successful parochial minister in the kingdom. Top that!

But Conyers' golden ministry was brought up short when
Luke 6:26 suddenly hit him between the eyes, 'Woe unto you,
when all men shall speak well of you!' This was followed by an
Evangelical conversion of Pauline proportions, whose main
consequence was that all men no longer spoke well of this

minister, who now denied his former gospel and encouraged all his hearers to invest in the aforementioned bleeding Lamb as their only route to salvation. Conyers' hagiographer catches his bold Methodist preaching before Archbishop Drummond of York during his visitation at Malton in 1764:

> During his discourse the beclouded countenance of his clerical hearers indicated that the important doctrine of salvation by grace, which Conyers proved and enforced, was extremely offensive, and when the service was concluded they treated him with the most pointed disrespect. As he was in the street in conversation with several farmers, the Archbishop advanced and accosted him as follows: 'Well, Conyers, you have given us a fine sermon!'
>
> 'I'm glad,' he replied, 'That it meets the approbation of Your Grace.'
>
> 'Approbation, approbation,' the Archbishop exclaimed, 'If you go on preaching such stuff you will drive all your parish mad. Were you to inculcate the morality of Socrates it would do more good than canting about the new birth.' His Grace immediately walked off without waiting for a reply.

But Conyers went on preaching such stuff, and at one service gathered a legendary 1800 communicants, quite a crowd for our 300-capacity church. When he announced he was to leave Helmsley for Deptford in 1776, many devoted parishioners threatened to lay themselves along the road, so that his carriage could only depart over their dead bodies. He cannily left by the dead of night, while his pickets lay slumbering in their beds rather than on the York Road.

Ten years on, John Newton preached a 7000-word sermon at Conyers' funeral, describing his friend in Christ-like terms, unequalled and inimitable, 'Did not our hearts burn within us when he talked with us on the road?' Yet his ministry was immensely costly. Newton points out that martyrs on the rack suffered less than Conyers did at the prospect of preaching. A stranger in the congregation, especially one he suspected was ordained, almost rendered him speechless. When prevailed upon to preach at the Archdeacon's visitation at Dartford, for the first few minutes in the pulpit, Conyers was driven blind with terror.

A terror matched with an Advent shiver as I closed the book's yellowing pages, pondering how, in just one tiny verse of Scripture, Christ had come to my predecessor and overturned his world. Long ago real giants deeply wailed in Helmsley, before whom I and even Charles Gray are mere croaking grasshoppers.

🍂 Monday, 1st December

The Advent hymn was barked out by a gale of tenor voices, suffused with the odd alto or soprano. The occasion? A gathering of all York Diocesan clergy in the chilliest York Minster to mark the Church's New Year. Archbishop David Hope quoted some words of his predecessor, Cosmo Gordon Lang, as apt for an over-busy world poised on the brink of 1998 as they were seventy years ago:

> I look back to the beginning of my time as Archbishop
> of York and think of all the hopes and plans with
> which I began. And now, after twenty years, the
> ending. Certainly there was enough and to spare of

doing. Yet, after all the ceaseless process of doing, what was actually done? Church life somewhat encouraged and invigorated, I hope ... but how many souls were brought nearer to God by all this doing? The words of the Methodist hymn come to mind, 'Doing is a deadly thing.' What is certain is that much more of true value might have been born if I had cared less for doing and more for being. If the inner life had been kept more true, the outer life would have born more fruit. "He that abides in me and me in him," says our Lord, "brings forth much fruit. For cut off from me you can do nothing." '

🍂 *Sunday, 7th December*

During Advent I cycled four of the numerous paths to Rievaulx's Cistercian abbey, two miles WNW of Helmsley. On a Sunday, as I rush between services, I puff up the B road, which climbs out of Helmsley before making the sharpest of wooded descents into Rievaulx. Motorcyclists from Middlesbrough, who pretend the road is a TT circuit, scream past me. Sadly too many never arrive or never return and our *sursum corda*s are accompanied by ambulance sirens.

A secret route is to cycle NNW out of Helmsley along the bottom of the steep-sided Beckdale, sneaking through Lord Feversham's pheasant pounds, the avian equivalent of a High Security Unit. At the pounds' end I wash my bicycle in the eponymous beck, the mudguards clogged with guano from the 30,000 frightened pheasants that roost here – 29,000 to be murdered annually, with 1000 spared to breed next year's kill. Keepers tell me that pheasants, with the lowest intelligence to total mass ratio in the animal kingdom, deserve to be shot. It would be interesting to apply this admirable principle to cull any sundry church organisation whose mass far exceeded its intelligence.

A perverse route is south, along the River Rye through Duncombe Park, Lord Feversham's estate, where on a frosty December morning the meadows crunch beneath my wheels. At the Cascades, the torrent plunges over a six-foot waterfall; apparently in summer they are all but dry and one can gingerly walk across them, but to do so now would mean I would be swiftly swept downstream to Malton. Many parishioners sneak into the park when his Lordship isn't looking and throw the ashes of their nearest and dearest into these waters. I'm rather taken with this modern-day Viking funeral where the deceased's voyage bisects Yorkshire, joining the Derwent above Kirkham Priory, meandering past the heathlands of York's vale, briefly flirting with the Ouse before being swept out to the North Sea by the Humber at Spurn Spit. As I pause by the Cascades I recall the Victorian diarist, Francis Kilvert's list of sleeping friends whose funerals he had taken '... Emily Banks, John Hatherwell, Limpedy Buckland, the gypsy girl, and many more'. I think of my many more, and bow my head.

Another perverse route is north out of Helmsley, climbing to the bleakest peak of the moors, where I turn west along the cliff-top, concentrating on steering as my bicycle cracks the ice on black pools of standing water and judders over the rockiest of paths. I dare to turn my head right for an instant and catch sight of pretty Bilsdale, once again realising that heaven will be a bit of a comedown after such breathtaking beauty.

What was formerly the drovers' road to Stockton-on-Tees is now a mere track to just four middle-of-nowhere farms. At one farm, the ram was in with the ewes, suffering the indignity of having had a canister strapped to his underside. The canister dribbles permanent turquoise ink, making him leave his mark on every ewe he mounts. I noted an impressive number of turquoise-backed ewes, as well as a couple of turquoise fence posts. The turquoise ewes had a fazed look. Those still pure-grey had darting eyes, simultaneously apprehensive and disappointed that they'd yet to be picked for the ram's team. The ram himself had the weary gait and bad temper of a cabinet minister who suddenly realises that even his stealthiest liaison is open to public gaze.

For me, all roads in these parts lead to a Eucharist in Rievaulx, where my venerable predecessor, Canon David Senior, felt there was a spiritual steam train behind him whenever he celebrated. Apparently Desmond Tutu, as a curate in London, concluded Midnight Mass by going out to dance in the churchyard, shouting 'Whoopee!' for sheer joy that God had become man. They'll be my cue on Christmas morning, as I speed down Rievaulx's bank and shout 'Whoopee!' before braking for my little congregation, patiently waiting to greet their Saviour in bread and wine.

Monday, 8th December

Christmas preparations are in full swing, including a discussion at December's Church Council, which had shades of the *Vicar of Dibley* about it. Inevitably the discussion turned to Christmases past, including one year when thieves broke into the church vestry on Christmas Eve and tried to jemmy open the safe containing the silver plate and chalice. 'The vestry had to be closed until the new year,' one stalwart informed us. 'It was in a terrible mess, but the police wanted everything left as it was until the forensic team had taken fingerprints. And then the place had to be sealed because they discovered asparagus all over the show.'

'Asparagus?' I asked, incredulously.

'Yeah, it all spilled out of the safe door when they tried to jemmy it open,' the stalwart assured me. 'Asparagus everywhere.'

'No, it wasn't asparagus, it was asbestos, you silly clot,' someone corrected her.

'Now,' I pronounced, taking my opportunity to bring the meeting back on task, 'I thought we'd do three new things for Christmas this year. First, let's have Ryedale School in for their carol concert. Secondly, let's have a Midnight Mass. Finally, let's have a crib service on Christmas Eve afternoon.'

The Church Council to a man and a woman couldn't have looked more shocked if I'd liberally scattered asparagus or even asbestos all over the place. But to their credit they gave me their unanimous support. They were pleased that I had got so involved in the schools so quickly, and they wanted to live out the welcoming mission statement we had agreed at the start, that God's so priceless he comes free.

In fact the Church Council, who must have been privately appalled at this young whippersnapper trying to shake them up, publicly gave me nothing but encouragement. It was those on the edge of church life, a small minority of people I termed 'Out-of-work U-boat commanders looking for a war', who could be relied upon to give me the flak, their voices and my replies strangely redolent of Jesus' temptations in the wilderness:

'But the school will make a mess, and they'll want to place their brass band in the sanctuary. Vicar Gray would turn in his grave with all those euphoniums and trombones, not to mention the drums. You'll destroy the sacredness of the place with their jingle bells and Santa's sleigh. And the kids and their parents never darken our doors for the rest of the year. Why should we welcome them now?'

'Because they're my friends, and Jesus welcomed children and so should we. And I'll be there to make sure they behave themselves and clear up any mess.'

'What do you want a crib service for, nobody will come? And the children will misbehave and start eating sweets and throwing things. Not like my children when they were young. They sat still and you wouldn't have heard a whisper from them ...'

'Oh, I like children in church and I don't mind if they're noisy. After all, a baby's cry piercing Bethlehem's night two thousand years ago started the whole thing off, broke history in two, BC/AD, so not a bad visual aid.'

'What do you want a Midnight Mass for? People are too old in Helmsley to stay up until that hour. You'll only get the drunken lot from the hotels, nobody else will be there.'

'Actually, I've invited the Methodists. They're unlikely to be drunk.'

'Methodists, what are you doing inviting them? They're not Church of England. I'm going to complain to the Bishop ...'

🍃 *Tuesday, 9th December*

'Story of Wise Men has historical basis!' At least that was the intention of my Advent house group, but it was nearly wrecked by the surprise visitation of the local RC priest. As well as discovering radical New Testament scholarship at an advanced age, he had recently attended a (Roman) Catholic Alpha. This made for a heady cocktail which gave his pronouncements an infallibility which brooked no discussion. 'You see,' he explained, like a genial grandfather correcting an all-too-naive grandchild, 'the Infancy Narratives only crop up in two Gospels. They were written very late on – the earliest Gospel makes no mention of them at all. It's the resurrection that really counts. We should stop putting Jesus into his cradle and celebrate the risen man.' I shuddered as the rest of the group looked as if an oracle had spoken.

I can see that we'll have to be as secretive as Rave Party organisers in planning future groups, switching venues at the last minute, dodging from Helmsley catacomb to catacomb to stave off persecution by Rome. Except I'm rather fond of this particular Tiberian incarnation. During the recent troubles in the parish several Anglicans broached switching their allegiance, but were dissuaded by his wisdom. 'I see it like this,' he gently advised them. 'We Roman Catholics and Anglicans are like two faith-families. All families have their problems. When such times come you don't drop your own family in favour of another one. You stay with them through the darkness until dawn breaks.' One can put up with a bit of demythologising in the face of such a generous ecumenical spirit.

🍃 *Thursday, 18th December*

'Keep to t' roads, Vicar,' the local butcher advised. He had recently watched the video, *An American Werewolf in London*, where the hound's victims unwisely stray onto the dark moors. I had stolen back from Whitby to lead the liveliest of carol services for our local comprehensive, complete with trombones, euphoniums and drums, but mercifully no Vicar Gray gyrating in his grave. With snowy weather closing in, the return journey over the moors would not be easy. I was even wondering about walking the Heartbeat railway line, which snakes through the valleys between Pickering and the coast, until the butcher put me off. So instead I nervously drove at 15 mph with blizzards raging and the road barely visible, the North York Moors like another world in which the Fylingdales' Pyramid seemed entirely apt as a white sandstorm swirled around it. It was the Saltersgate Inn, empty and lightless beneath the Moors' saddle, which jarred, an epitome of utter desolation. I was so very relieved when the twinkling lights of Whitby came into view; even more relieved when I safely reached the Priory just after midnight, to find the sisters had put a hot water bottle in my bed, and left out a flask of hot milk to welcome me home.

I was braving three days in the resort of Whitby in order to lead a retreat at Sneaton Castle, the mother house of the OHP nuns (which staffs the outpost at Rievaulx), with a statue of St Hilda, a local seventh-century girl made exceedingly good, overlooking my every address. Wild weather racked Whitby, the seas high, little boats and not-so-little boats reeling to and fro, their bows at times vertical. While the storm beat on my window-pane, the priory was amazingly calm, the round of worship superb, excellence combined with a lightness of touch, where I was the only bass in a world where the treble clef was queen. The sisters seemed so alive, a twinkle in their eyes and their conversations theologically astute. Every day they listened intently over lunch to Radio Four's *World at One*, seasoning their faith with a canny knowledge of the way the world was and an acute alertness to the points where that world was hurting. It was me, the retreat conductor, who came away refreshed, encouraged that at least this religious Order was in good heart, standing as a counter sign of contemplation against a hyperactive earth.

I suppose it's amazing that I enjoy retreats, given that I was dragged along to a parish retreat at the age of seven. No one saw fit to tell me that the retreat was a silent one, and I was bewildered why none of the surly looking adults would talk to me. Adult not talking to adult came as no surprise – our East Hull congregation seemed to be always falling out and bombarding each other with a sulky silence.

Wydale Hall, York's Diocesan Retreat House, is set in the most forlorn part of the North York Moors, where the sounds of the countryside surprised little urban me as much as the silence of the adults. It's difficult to put into words how simultaneously perplexing and wonderful it is for a child to hear a pheasant call for the first time in his life.

In those far-off days the OHP nuns ran Wydale, and one novice took pity on my lonely plight and taught me to gather and play conkers. Forty years on, I still come across her at tediously serious diocesan events and catch her eye, the gleam in which betrays she would have much preferred to have spent a lifetime playing conkers with a chestnut-haired little boy. Mind you, every nun seems to have that look ...

Maybe it has something to do with the confessional at Sneaton Castle, which is housed next door to a lavatory, with only a thin partition wall in between the two. In order that a private time should not be invaded by the sound of the water pipes, and, more importantly, so that any intimate conversations would not be overheard by an eavesdropper lingering in the loo, before any confession began I had to leave my quivering penitent and attempt to lock the lavatory from the outside.

This I did by inserting my little finger into the bolt housing, pushing the 'vacant' sign to 'engaged'. It took me only a few minutes to extract my finger, and by the end of the lengthy confession it had almost stopped throbbing, its red pulse hardly perceptible when wrapped in a purple stole.

Unlocking the loo from the outside proved far harder than locking it. Like a tiny rodent snug in its winter den, the bolt refused to be coaxed out of its housing and after several unsuccessful attempts, and several quizzical looks from passing nuns, I gave up, leaving the lavatory sealed, like the confessional, for ever.

❧ Thursday, 25th December

Fortunately my crib service featuring the world premier of *Thomas the Tank Engine comes to Bethlehem* brought the house down, and a packed house at that. Shocked purists, be reassured that it wasn't as bad as it could have been. There was no 'And the Angel Daisy said unto Thomas, "Hail, Thomas, full of steam, the Fat Controller is with thee ..." ' I simply told the story of Thomas on tour, ending up at Bethlehem, dreaming of being greeted at the stable by a Christ laughing at his antics. I hoped the children would dream such dreams of Christ cheering them on Christmas night.

Lord Feversham was the star of the show for the traditional bit, reading the story of the coming of the Wise Men from Matthew's Gospel. As was his wont, averse as he was to anything modern where Church was concerned, my Lord read about the birth of Our Lord from the Authorised Version, and he proved the meanest Herod I have ever heard. When he read, 'Go and search diligently for the young child, and when ye have found him, bring me word again, that I may come and worship him also,' he sounded so utterly sinister that a chill as cold as ice broke into our warm Christmas festivities and made all of us shiver.

My mistake was to get the youngsters in the congregation to impersonate a Bethlehem flock of sheep. One toddler's baas were incessant, a crescendo which accompanied the rest of my story. His twin wasn't caught by the sheep bug at all, giving his brother increasingly disdainful looks hardly worthy of the coming of the Prince of Peace.

I dread such chaos, and had to lie down following the crib service to recover, yet people rave about such services. Almost as if they are affirmed when the chaos of their own lives is met by chaos in church. I was really touched that later on Christmas Eve a young mother brought me a box of chocolates. She clearly felt out of her depth coping with her new-born baby – who wouldn't? But the fact that she'd felt welcomed without reservation at the crib service, surrounded by other people out of their depth (including me), somehow affirmed her and made her deeply grateful. And the Word became chaos and dwelt amongst us.

'The best thing Anglicans and Methodists can do together is to drive each other to celebrate their particular denomination,' an old lay preacher once advised me. This gem sprang to mind minutes before the Midnight Mass. I had arrived in church over an hour earlier, in theory to give me space for reflection and prayer. In practice I spent the time lighting every possible candle in case the howling gales off the moor brought the power lines down. My serving team had retired early, so it was left to me to stoke up the thurible as precious seconds ticked by. I decided to encourage smouldering charcoal with a generous dose of methylated spirits, which instantly converted the dying embers to a blazing furnace whose flames licked the vestry roof. As I huffed and puffed to blow the thing out, I caught the eye of my Methodist colleague, whose congregation were joining us for the service. Her look exuded immense gratitude that she was as she was and not an Anglican. Another triumph for ecumenism.

Despite the midnight fireworks, at least we were spared the drunken hoards that my critics so generously predicted. Our Christmas morning communions were pure magic, with a little boy demonstrating his super-charged car up and down the aisle during my sermon, shocking the out-of-work U-boat commanders but delighting the rest of the congregation.

Following that service at Helmsley, I simply didn't have the time to scrape the ice off my car (there had been the heaviest of frosts followed by snow showers) so I set off for Rievaulx on my bike, slithering down the icy bankside, wheels like skis, legs like ski poles. As I dropped into the hamlet, the low clouds cleared and the sun shone brilliantly, the lines of the ruined abbey highlighted by snow. The church, formerly the abbey's slipper chapel, was warm and full of expectant people, serenaded by a silver band who greeted my arrival by striking up 'Jingle Bells', complete with sleigh bells. I unpacked the robes from my frost-rimmed rucksack, but found my white stole must have blown out as I sped down Rievaulx's bank. I just had to trust its absence didn't make the Communion invalid, any more than 'Jingle Bells' presence made it invalid. In fact, it was such an intensely joyful gathering that I sensed the Cistercian monks had risen out of their frozen graves and were singing with us; although perhaps *Adeste Fideles* rather than 'Jingle Bells'. As I cycled back up the 1:4 bank afterwards, there was my white stole, tastefully draped around a holly tree; after all 'The holly and the ivy' is probably the most priestly of carols, celebrated by R. S. Thomas:

> This Christmas before
> an altar of gold
> the holly will remind
> us how love bleeds.

> *(Residues, 2002, p. 47)*

As I pedalled back to Canons Garth and barred my vicarage door against all-comers, Parson Woodforde's ghost came to shame me. I recently took a register of the 26 Christmases Woodforde diarised at Weston Longville in Norfolk from 1776 to 1801, where he entertained without fail half a dozen poor old men to Christmas dinner. Though frail, many actually have the longevity of my sick communicants, and rally to attend year after year; such as Tom Carr, who turned up for a record 17 Christmas dinners. Over the years Woodforde's largesse augments the standard fare of boiled beef and plum pudding: in 1782 mince pies are added; half a pint of strong beer apiece in 1784; boiled rabbit and even a woman, Widow Case, in 1793: prior to that it had been a male-only domain, with Woodforde sending the old men home with a shilling for their wives.

Neither epileptic faints in church, nor ice all under foot, nor extreme bad walking, nor 'his foot extremely painful' (a frequent complaint), ever separates Woodforde from cherishing Christmas dinner. 'It pleased me so much to see the old folks so happy as they were,' he notes in 1792. Bidding his diners farewell in 1783, he writes, 'Pray God, ever continue to me the power of doing good.' And so pray all of us.

🖎 Sunday, 28th December

'A cold coming we had of it,' is the chilly start to T. S. Eliot's poem, *Journey of the Magi*. A cold coming I had of it too. The weather forecast had been dire: sub-zero temperatures, heavy snowfall, winds gusting in from the Arctic, all conspiring against my Holy Innocents' Day Eucharist at East Moors, five miles up the bleak North York Moors. I made the lonely journey by bicycle, with chalice and paten, wine and bread and all other necessary ingredients for a communion packed into my rucksack. Usually cycling up 1:3 hills dispels the cold, but not today: the chill bitterness of the journey was unrelenting. The streams which normally tumbled down the hillsides had become ice and crept across the road like mini-glaciers. In the middle of the lane lay a rabbit, as stiff as a board. Her body was perfect – she hadn't been hit by traffic or attacked by a bird of prey, I guess the cold had simply got to her and her arteries had frozen solid. I stopped and moved her body to the verge, kicking the cold soil from a rock-like molehill to cover her with earth: it seemed a more tender funeral than being mashed by the wheels of a passing car.

Not that there were any passing cars. I skated over the ford and arrived at the little church so celebrated by Betjeman, and set up for the service, wondering if anyone else at all was going to come. One person did, explaining that she had watched me descend the slipperiest Cow House Bank before she had decided it was safe for her to follow in her four-by-four. Another family joined our celebration half way through, and so boosted the *sursum corda* (it can be so disheartening when you say 'The Lord be with you,' and no one replies!), our breath condensing before us like clouds of incense. When it came to the administration, I lifted the tiny chalice to my lips, but no wine came out. Even the alcohol had turned to gel in these polar temperatures, so I cupped my hand around the frozen grail to thaw out God, a priestly role if ever there was one.

Why didn't I cancel the service? Because I had promised a mother whose son had tragically died on that day two years earlier that I would pray for him out here, and I could hardly let her down, with a cheery, 'So sorry, it was a bit icy, so we called it off.' I'm never too happy about letting God down either: 'Thanks, God, for struggling to Bethlehem and Calvary and all stops in between, but it was a bit slippery underfoot today, so Holy Communion was scrapped.'

On the cycle ride home I huffed and puffed up Cow House Bank. A deer scrambled down the hill, followed closely by her fawn and crossed the road in front of me. It seemed almost as if they nodded to me before they disappeared once again into the dark forest, making it a morning for lost children and found children.

Monday, 29th December

Perhaps my coldest journey was today's to York for a cremation where there were no mourners, other than the funeral directors and me. One of the risks of having a service in church followed by a 30-mile trek to the nearest crematorium is that you lose a congregation en route. 'Although I never met the deceased,' that hoary preface to so many tedious funeral homilies, was not quite appropriate this time. While as a priest and adult I had certainly never encountered him, as a child I had, when thirty years previously I visited Helmsley with my parents searching for a new organ for our village church. They were delighted to come across a harmonium in pristine condition. 'How much do you want for it?' my father asked the vendor.

'Oh, four to five pounds,' he replied.

'Well, that seems a good price,' my father responded, eager to make the deal. 'Let's say four pounds ten shillings.'

The vendor looked puzzled for a moment, before he bellowed, 'No, no, not four to five pounds, you didn't hear me right. I said forty five pounds.' Despite the 1000% inflation, my father bought the instrument, which was duly transported back to the Vale of York on a farm truck. Then I never saw the man again until I gazed at his lonely coffin three decades on. 'There is always one moment in childhood when a door opens and lets the funeral in,' to parody Graham Greene.

'How much do you want for travel expenses?' the undertaker asked me afterwards.

'Four to five pounds,' I replied, smiling. Understandably he didn't get the joke.

Part Two

1998: New Year to Good Friday

🍂 *Friday, 2nd January*

Over Christmas I heard Alan Bennett's bleak account of the descent of his mother through depression and dementia to oblivion. Though what Bennett had to say jarred with all the tinsel and Christmas heartiness, yet his honesty, insight and courage to tell this saddest of stories straight spoke powerfully to me. It should be compulsory hearing for every priest who encounters mental illness and deterioration; or alternatively just chairs a PCC.

Actually, nearly all psychiatric/geriatric wards surprise me with a very strong sense of holiness. Such places are hardly peaceful: folk thrash about, bully, shout incessantly, fights take place, accompanied by inappropriate music blaring out. I cower in a corner, holding the hand of the person I am visiting. This is probably as bad as it can get, everybody's nightmare. Yet there is a holy sense of relief that you're not on the outside avoiding it, but have arrived in its midst and have no fall to fear.

Even the inevitable irrational conversations and comments in such places soothe rather than faze me, warmly redolent of supervisions and university sermons and philosophy of religion seminars at Cambridge, where I nodded and tried to look wise, but actually hardly understood a word. One philosophy seminar proved a rare exception, where the Chairman congratulated Rowan Williams on his engagement to be married. He then looked ashamed at this rare lapse into lucid humanity, quickly reverting to the usual philosophy-babble.

Bennett is irked by the cheeriness and familiarity of staff on the psychiatric ward, though realises that he, not them, is the problem. 'They know they are in a *Carry On* film. I am playing it like it's *Brief Encounter*.' Yet when I visited it today, Malton's geriatric unit presented me with the best picture of grace I have ever encountered. An attendant, whose skin was as black as jet, was playing dominoes with an old dear with her grey hair in a bun. She was clumsy, kept dropping her dominoes; he was patient, ever picking and re-picking them up. Eventually the game came to a conclusion. 'You've won!' the attendant announced to a packed room where only I was listening. 'You're a world champion, Maisie, nobody can beat you at dominoes.' Maisie's face shone with pride, positively beatific.

🍂 Tuesday, 6th January

Premises inappropriately designed, compounded by a raw chill; tuneless songs, sung half-heartedly; tedious, joyless activities, a travesty of the dizzy heights which could be achieved elsewhere: no, not a Church of England service but a session at our local playgroup. We have an ordinand of high promise on placement with us, so I feel obliged to live out the implications of the incarnation and engage with every organisation in the parish. Mind you, had St Paul ever encountered a nursery, I don't think he would have waxed so lyrical about nothing in all creation separating us from the love of God.

My heart went out to a 2-year-old girl who sobbed continually, grieving for her missing mother. The playgroup leader was impressively shrewd in her analysis: 'You see, she's Basque-French and they speak French all the time at home. That's her language of comfort. However soothing our English, she sees it as harsh and alien and so we do nothing more than aggravate her.'

My imagination ran riot, heavily influenced by Dennis Potter's *The Singing Detective,* where the play's anti-hero, Philip Marlow, constrained to a hospital bed with psoriatic arthritis has the weirdest morphine-induced delusions and fantasies. In my mind's eye the playgroup helpers started swaying their broad hips as they crooned the banned 1960s single 'Je t'aime' to placate the Basque child's tears, other children taking a break from anarchy for a few moments to provide the orchestral back-up.

The theological side of my brain ran along a different tack. What harsh sounds do we offer to all the grieving, inwardly sobbing adults who come to church? How can a liturgy couched in the style which is a cross between a Cambridge Tripos essay and a Shakespearean soliloquy speak comfortable words to them? I concocted a homely dialect mass to address their condition:

> T' Lord's 'ere:
>
> *Aye, 'e is that lad (lass* if the celebrant is a woman).
> Lift up thy 'earts:
> *I'm only lifting up me 'eart if it's to t' Lord.*
> Fair enough. Let's give thanks to t' Lord our God.
> *Eeh, it's reet to give 'im thanks and praise.*
> Now cum on lads and lasses, it's not only reet, it's our duty and joy ...

On second thoughts, I think I prefer 'Je t'aime'. After all, Bishop John Robinson, at the *Lady Chatterley* trial, did liken sexual intercourse to holy communion (strictly lower case); although I can't say it's a parallel that leaps to mind as I gaze at a typical Anglican congregation.

🍂 *Sunday, 11th January*

At the hamlet chapel at Rievaulx, the water provided for cleansing the vessels after communion had a distinctly fusty flavour, and drinking it on successive weeks made me feel giddy. It could be that they just haven't changed the water for ages, or that they've drawn it from the spring of clearish water which spurts out by the roadside. Many locals will drink nothing else, turning a blind eye to the dead sheep marinading in the spring's source higher up the bank. My lifelong acquaintance with the Church of England has taught me that complaining about even such trivial things can cause the deep and lasting offence on which reformations thrive, so I resolved on my own secret solution. This week I hid a flask of water in my trouser pocket (no Mae West jokes, please) and at the appropriate moment, with my back turned to the congregation, employed a sleight of hand to make sure I had fresh, if by this time rather warm, water for the ablutions. My cunning plan went slightly wrong in that the flask leaked, so that my procession around the church was marked by a slug-like trail dribbling from my sock. But even so, the fact that I had avoided being poisoned compensated for any embarrassment.

The incident brought to mind William Fitzherbert, the ill-fated twelfth-century Archbishop of York. On his appointment, his triumphal entry into the city was marred when the weight of clergy setting out to greet him caused the wooden bridge over the Ouse to collapse, but miraculously without any loss of life. His luck was short-lived, however, in that he was prematurely despatched when a piqued Archdeacon of York, serving at a Mass at which his Archbishop was celebrating, slipped poison into the communion wine. I thank God that whatever the modern Church's faults, at least some things have improved since that murderous twelfth century. Even so, in my former job as Archbishop of York's chaplain, my boss always took particular pains to make sure that whenever he celebrated communion before the York Diocesan Senior Staff Meeting, it was trusty old me who served, with all the archdeacons safely confined to the choir stalls.

● *Wednesday, 21st January*

Home communions today. I start the morning with a mid-week communion in church with about a dozen communicants, where I consecrate enough bread to distribute to the housebound following the service, so that the housebound are in a real sense the wider congregation. Clergy of yesteryear could get very up-tight about taking the sacrament on tour, as they went on their home communion rounds, wearing the pyx (the little silver box which contains the sacrament) around their neck, resolutely refusing to talk to a soul. Some even expected any soul they came across to genuflect before them. This somewhat precious habit was turned on its head by Archbishop Desmond Tutu who observed that as he went around his parish as a priest, he was the one who felt like genuflecting before every person he encountered, because each and every one was a tabernacle of the Christ who dwells within all God's children. Frank Weston, Bishop of Zanzibar, was the darling of the Anglo-Catholic movement yet had some very firm things to say to his constituency to save them from a piety which was hopelessly introspective, such as, 'It's no use worshipping Christ in the Tabernacle if you can't pity Him in the slum.' Home communions are a two-way process, both taking Christ out but also being met by him, in all his marvellousness and also in all his quirkiness.

At my first port of call, I end up wrestling on the carpet with a large dog. 'We rescued him from a RSPCA pound,' his owner explained. 'He obviously likes you.' I managed to extricate myself from the creature's jaws, convinced that in an earlier incarnation he must have been maltreated by a cleric. 'I prefer Border terriers myself,' I said, as I futilely tried to brush pints of doggy saliva off my cassock. Despite my embracing a ministry of close encounter, I was beginning to see how those priests of yesteryear who kept their distance had their point.

'Oh, they can be very difficult dogs,' my communicant replied, dismissively. 'I heard of one that kept worrying sheep. In the end they had to put it …'

'Down?!' I interrupted, supplying the dread word of doom.

'No, they had to put it in with t' ram. It never worried sheep again after that.'

I gave a knowing smile. From time to time I have to act the ram with those loveable human terriers who develop an annoying habit of worrying Christ's flock.

Next a visit to a housebound couple, who tell me how their kindly neighbour fetches them fish and chips, the order always correct: deaf and dumb, he has to make signs to sundry shop assistants.

A recently widowed woman next, with sympathy cards thronging her lounge. We talk about the big society wedding which had all but coincided with her husband's funeral, in particular the megabucks fireworks display at the evening reception, with rockets bursting into coloured lights, showering her husband's grave. She had watched it all in her little garden, arm around her daughter – 'Eeh, it were a grand send off for him!'

Next to the home of another couple, where the husband has suffered stroke after debilitating stroke, and clearly has only days left to live. 'It's no good giving him communion, Vicar,' his wife advises me. 'He can't swallow anything solid.'

'Can you get me a cup of water and a teaspoon?' The woman gets up and moves slowly to the kitchen, giving me a bit of a quizzical look. 'Have you come over faint, Vicar,' she asks, as she returns complete with a cup filled to the brim.

'No, I'm fine, just leave the cup on the coffee table and we'll start the service.' When it came to the point for receiving communion, I took a teaspoon of water and popped the tiniest morsel of consecrated wafer on it before feeding it to my communicant. He swallowed, and then clearly wanted to say something, but the words took ages to come out, which they did eventually: 'Thank you, thank you,' he uttered, from the very depth of his being.

As we chatted afterwards, the woman told me about her brother, recuperating (or recruiting as they say in these parts) after surgery. Unable to do any manual labour himself, he unsuccessfully tried to cajole a firm of agricultural engineers to dig his wayward hedge. But one fresh-faced worker offered to do the job in his lunch hour, and did it well, working like a Trojan. 'What's your name, then?' the invalid asked.

'Tatton Sykes,' the youngster replied. 'Father wants me to see the real world before I take over the estate.' His Victorian forebear, also called Tatton Sykes, had cultivated the wild Yorkshire Wolds, hundreds of square miles of them, so clearing a few yards of hedge clearly was a doddle for his descendant. And the Wold was made flesh and dwelt amongst us.

Sunday, 25th January

For the week of Prayer for Christian Unity, Evensong at Helmsley Church was kicked into touch, and instead we were invaded by the Stalinist local council of churches, who insisted on doing their own thing in their way, irrespective of All Saints' tradition, let alone mine. I was shunted out of the way into the sanctuary on the wrong side of a screen onto which sundry interminable choruses were projected. Half the congregation sang their hearts out and then sang them out again, the other (indigenous) half kept their lips pursed and looked distinctly bored.

Although I have always been intrigued by Leonardo da Vinci's mirror writing, I am not sufficiently fluent to translate at the speed which singing requires. Nor did I want to look like

John Redwood at a Welsh Eisteddfod, standing there miming inappropriately and looking like an utter pillock.

Fortunately the Lord (as he is known by the half of the congregation singing their hearts out) came to my rescue and drew my eyes to the memorial tablet opposite me. Any space on Helmsley's church walls not daubed with Vicar Gray's murals is taken up with sundry memorials to local worthies, seeming giants to our grasshoppers. Usually I give them and all the genealogy cranks a wide berth, observing Mark Twain's dictum, 'Ask not who your great grandfather was; rather ask who his great grandson is going to be.' But tonight I was deeply grateful for the words of the memorial opposite me, since they fitted exactly the tune we were trilling at that moment, Graham Kendrick's, 'The Servant King:'

> Here lieth Robert Dixon,
> For forty years vicar of this parish.
> And his wife Elizabeth,
> Who-o-o-o survived him.
> Erected by
> Grateful parishioners
> In loving me-e-e-mory
> Of a faithful and devoted ministry
> Which benefited them all.

Strangely enough, the words fitted other tunes too, so I was able to sing my heart out throughout. 'Eeh, it's so good to see a minister enjoying t' choruses like you enjoyed 'em tonight!' a Methodist lay preacher commented to me at the service's eventual end. I nodded sagely and let my silence be taken as agreement. It would be four years before our turn came around again to host the ecumenical roadshow, by which time either I would have mastered mirror-writing, or left.

🍂 *Wednesday, 4th February*

More home communions, starting with Betty, a very gracious but very ill lady, whose husband, Neil, was a retired vet who in his working life had gathered enough stories of being t' local vetin'ry to give James Herriot a run for his money. Their house and grounds were a veritable menagerie of horses, cats, geese, ducks, chickens and sundry fowl. A guinea pig colony of indeterminate size roams free on their lawn, with guinea pigs escaping now and again and being returned by neighbours who find them nestling in their vegetable patch.

This loveliest of couples never allow me to depart empty handed, with a box of half a dozen eggs always stuffed into the case which contained my robes and the Blessed Sacrament. Until you cracked the eggs open, you were never quite sure of their origin, whether they were from a big chicken or a small goose and all birds in between.

Today following communion, as we sat chatting around their Aga in their homely kitchen, they told me the sorry tale of their most recent animal addition, two deerhound puppies. One had sadly contracted double pneumonia and despite Neil's ministrations clearly hadn't got long for this world; the other was pining away as she watched her sister die, eating and drinking nothing, hastening her own death.

I asked to see them and was ushered into the utility room, where two deerhound puppies the size of ponies were lying in their baskets, looking in the sorriest of states. The puppy with double pneumonia was on a drip, and pathetically lifted up its huge paw which I took in my hand. I felt both moved by their plight, and angry that a present intended to bring Betty a glimpse of life in her final days had only brought more death. Totally on the spur of the moment, in a sort of crazed spirit of righteous indignation, I prayed that the puppy would be healed and bring us joy. Neil the vet, who had seen countless animals live and die, gave me a kindly but curious look. It was an impetuous act, muddled theologically but driven by my desire to see life where only death was on the cards; I was supposed to be a minister of the resurrection, after all! And of all animals, there's something about dogs which champions the Christian virtues of loyalty and friendship, sentiments no doubt driving this little ditty by Father Potter of Peckham:

> I wonder if Christ had a little brown dog,
> One he felt was a pal, like mine.
> With long silky ears and a nose soft and wet,
> and eyes brown and tender that shine.
> I don't think he did, because I read,
> 'Alone in the Garden he prayed,
> When disciples and friends had left him and fled.'
> I feel sure that his dog would have stayed ...

I didn't stay any longer, but made my excuses and left with my eggs. Later that night, Neil rang me to say that the puppy, against all expectations, had rallied, and because she was picking up, her pining sister was rallying too. 'Perhaps the antibiotics you were injecting her with finally kicked in,' I said. I gabbled on to Neil about a former York Diocesan Senior Staff meeting at Bishopthorpe when we were told about a clergy wife who was suffering from acute arthritis. After having both gold injections from her consultant and also a famous evangelist lay hands on her for healing, her condition had miraculously improved. 'I put my money on the gold!' the Archbishop had joked.

'I don't think it was the antibiotics,' Neil concluded, 'so thank you, Vicar.' Ever a man of few words, with that he rang off.

Back to my home communion round, communion with Betty was confusingly followed by communion with another

Betty, who as a young girl had worked for the local railway company, prior to its closure in the 1950s. She told me of one perilous journey during the Second World War when she was travelling, inevitably by rail, to the company's headquarters in York. The previous night a German bomber had dropped a bomb on the railway line, which had left the line intact, but had blown away all the earth on the embankment beneath it. When Betty's train came along, the unsupported rails couldn't take the strain, and the whole train rolled off down the bankside, the flimsy wooden carriages splintering into matchwood and throwing Betty and her fellow passengers into the surrounding fields. Miraculously, bar a few cuts and bruises, no one was hurt. The whole group simply dusted themselves down and hobbled along the railway line a couple of miles to the junction with the East Coast line. There they alerted the signalman to the disaster before catching the next York-bound train, carry-on-as-normal being the order of their wartime day.

Clearly of the hardiest stock, Betty told me another wartime story with a far less happy outcome. There had been a Sunday School excursion from Helmsley to Scarborough and the day had gone deliriously well, the packed train disgorging its happy passengers at Helmsley station just before 11pm, way past everybody's bed-time in those days. The empty train had then continued to Ampleforth to park up for the night. The engine driver disconnected the coupling to the carriages, shouting to the guard to put the brake on, only to see the carriages roll away from him down the gradual incline towards Helmsley. He chased after the carriages until they came to a halt at the end of the incline and climbed into the guard's van to remonstrate with the guard, only to find him shot dead. Further investigation revealed that a stray Messerschmitt had strafed the train's carriages as it journeyed out of Helmsley. Had the Messerschmitt been a few minutes earlier or the train a few minutes later, then it would have taken out most of Helmsley's population.

Helmsley's railway dominates my day, in that following a funeral that afternoon, I got chatting to a distant relation of the deceased.

'Have you come far?' a well-dressed woman had asked him as he squeezed beside her in the pew.

'Yes, from Canada,' he drawled.

'So what connection do you have with the deceased?' she asked.

'We're distant cousins,' he replied. 'To cut a long story short, my great-grandfather was stationmaster at Helmsley at the turn of the last century.'

'Oh, how interesting,' the lady interrupted him. 'What a fine station to be in charge of.' Though the little branch line had only managed a couple of passenger trains a day, the station at Helmsley was indeed palatial, because of Lord Feversham's insistence that the place contain five waiting rooms, separate first class for both ladies and gentlemen, separate second class, with a fifth room for the rest.

'Well,' the Canadian continued, 'fine station it may well have been, but my great-granddad found it far from fine. One day he was ordered to hold the 9am York train for Lord Feversham. Nine o'clock came and went, and since there was no sign of his lordship, he let the train go. When Lord Feversham eventually arrived at the station, he was furious; since he was a director of the railway company, he had my great-grandfather dismissed. Great-granddad, fed up with the feudal state of things here, emigrated.'

'How very interesting,' the woman replied.

'And have you come far?' the man asked politely.

'No, I live here,' she replied, smiling sweetly. 'You see, I'm the present Lady Feversham!' Following which they had exchanged no further words.

Sunday, 8th February

The Song of Songs came up at Evensong tonight. Whenever I read the book, it shames my lack of sensuality, and I am embarrassed by my embarrassment. The most notorious occasion was in my former job as Archbishop's chaplain, when it was my turn to read the lesson in Bishopthorpe Chapel, the Archbishop the only member of the congregation. 'How beautiful you are, my dearest, how beautiful!' I stuttered before my distinctly unmoved boss. 'Your eyes are like doves ... your parted lips are like a pomegranate cut open ... your two breasts are like two fawns, twin fawns of a gazelle.' Archbishop Habgood was down to do the prayers; he was unfazed, simply giving God thanks for the marvellous gift of erotic love. If only all Primates were as at ease with the Song of Songs' subject matter.

I inadvertently typed tonight's lesson on the weekly bulletin as the Song of Snogs, a Freudian slip if ever there was one. It made me think of other lesson howlers I have giggled at during my few months in Helmsley. One reader startled our Evensong congregation by the following rendering of Joshua 3:10: 'This is how you will know the living God is among you, and that he will drive out before you the Canaanites, Hittites, Hivites, Perizzites, Girgashites, Amorites, and – *wait for it* – the Jesuits.' A misreading of Ezekiel 18:2 introduced another Evensong congregation to a previously untried delicacy, 'The fathers have eaten sewer grapes and the children's teeth are set on edge.' Another reader, relaying the exciting account of Jesus healing a multi-possessed man by casting out the spirits into a herd of swine, had the aforementioned spirits pleading, 'Do not send us to the abbess!' Mind you, abbesses I have known could be far fiercer than the abyss which was the spirits' eventual destination. A retired priest, who really should have known better, informed our congregation about a Caesarian woman (*a Hebrew midwife?*) who kept pestering Jesus to heal her possessed daughter. A woman who obviously had housework on her mind described God as hoovering over the abyss in the primeval scene in Genesis 1. Although, thinking about it, I rather like that picture of God, a hard-pressed 1950s housewife, continually hoovering up the mess we adolescents make of the world.

Talking of adolescents, my wife Rachel came across the ultimate howler when conducting a poll of her Year 11 RE group (fifth form in our day) as to who knew the words of the Lord's Prayer. 'Doesn't it begin "Our Father which aren't in heaven"?' one boy asked. It is good to know that there is at least one child out there who understands Paul Tillich and his Death of God theology.

Following Evensong as I recovered from yet another Sunday, I thumbed through a copy of Newton and Cowper's Olney hymns, published in 1779 by the same John Newton who had preached at the funeral of Helmsley's very own Richard Conyers. 'I really do need to get out more,' I thought, sensing that surfing 348 neo-Calvinist ditties wasn't the best way to relax of a Sunday evening. But soon the whole family were guffawing at a hymnbook which seemed to have been designed by Biggus Dickus of *Life of Brian* fame and thcreaming Violet Elizabeth, *Just William's* bête noire, brought about by the old English habit of writing *s* as *f*. Short phrases which leapt laughingly out of the page included: a thankful *fong*, *floth* and *fleep*, a leper's *cafe* and *fun* at noon. 'Is not my *cafe* amazing?' a surprisingly immodest Bartimaeus boasts to his friends. Birds manifold line up for Bartimaeus' menu: 'My *foul* has been in *fuch* a *cafe*' vied with 'Since at his feet my *foul* has *fat* ... "Art thou a *finner*, *foul*," he *faid*.' The ultimate tongue-twister was 'Phy*fician* of my *fin-fick foul*'. Yet once you have broken the code, humour gives way to poignancy: youngsters, 'young in years, old in *fin*' are harangued at the approach of New Year – no cosy Communion before confirmation with John Newton. ''Tis *ftrange* they *fhould refufe* to bathe, and yet frequent the pool,' he reflects

about the halt and lame who hung around Bethesda, simultaneously wondering why some tedious people frequent church but
fail to draw on Christ. His antidote? 'Let us now a ble*ff*ing *f*eek.'

Churches were full of people *f*eeking ble*ff*ings in those days,
eager for Olney's hymns with Su Doku and hilarity all rolled
into one. Lord Feversham is always on at me about making the
Elizabethan language in the Book of Common Prayer more
accessible to the young. Simply revert to printing *s* as *f*, and
you'll have *f*ick *f*apling *f*inners *f*urging into the ai*f*les. And every
one of them *f*o well behaved, not even *f*urreptitiously *f*ucking a
polo mint during a boring *f*ermon.

🍃 *Tuesday, 10th February*

A lady called at Canons Garth tonight to collect the Banns'
certificate for her son's forthcoming wedding. Headmistress of a
primary school about ten miles to the south of Helmsley, she
reminded me we had met before when in my previous job as
Archbishop's chaplain I had accompanied David Hope as he
conducted a *tour de force* through every deanery of his new
archdiocese, like an amiable suzerain enrolling his vassals.

I distinctly recalled the visit we had made to the lady's
school: a tiny Victorian building with two classrooms, high
ceilings and windows, peeling plaster, with just two teachers
and about thirty children. The displays were fresh, decking
every wall, covering up the cracks in the plaster. The children
were spick and span, scrubbed up specially for the archiepiscopal visit, looking the epitome of life in all its fullness. All except
one. Breaking away from the archiepiscopal roadshow, I peeped
behind a dingy curtain and discovered a 5-year-old boy lying on
a PE mat by a radiator, wrapped up in a rug, asleep. 'Epilepsy!'
someone whispers to me, in shocked tones. The tragedy was a
double one, in that his twin brother was epileptic too, with fits
taking turns between them.

Curiously enough that morning our Gospel reading had been about an epileptic boy who was healed by Jesus, after the disciples had tried their best but got absolutely nowhere with him. 'There is no means of casting out this sort but by prayer,' Jesus concludes. I remembered praying for the little fellow with all my heart and soul, but still he lay there, ashen. I felt bogus to the core.

Two years on, with the school's headmistress sitting before me in my Helmsley study, I asked after the poorly child. 'Oh, that Archbishop must have got something about him,' she exclaimed, 'because neither the boy nor his twin ever had a fit again.' Apparently she and her colleague had expected the illness to dominate the twins' school career, and had received hours of special training in how to cope. All to no avail because an archbishop had passed by.

🍂 Friday, 20th February

Our primary school had rave reviews following its production of *Joseph and the Amazing Technicolor Dreamcoat* last November, where little Laura stole the show. Today they built on their success by staging scenes from *The Sound of Music* in their community assembly in the school hall.

The Sound of Music is Laura's favourite film. In fact she is obsessed with it, knows every song, knows every scene, so she was a natural if unusual choice for Maria. Admittedly the school production in parts was at variance with the Julie Andrews blockbuster, with alps, abbeys and Nazis conspicuous by their absence. Nor was the production helped by Laura repeatedly wandering off mid-scene to raid the school lunch trolley for a snack.

But there is a moment in the story where Maria is torn between vocations, vocation to be a nun and vocation to be a wife and mother, and retreats to the Abbey, only to be sent packing by the Abbess trilling 'Climb every mountain'. Laura's return to the seven von Trapp children was highly dramatic to say the least. She ran at full pelt towards them, her face radiant with a positively beatific smile, and somehow managed to embrace all seven children and Captain von Trapp (a highly embarrassed boy in Year 6) simultaneously in her little arms. In all the theatre I have witnessed, I have never seen such an action so epitomize sheer love and sheer joy. It was nothing less than love-incarnate performed before our eyes, our tear-filled eyes, as every parent in the audience wished they were capable of loving just a tenth as fiercely as little Laura. Her face shone like an angel's face. Which was ironic really, because in Japan children with Down's syndrome are called angels.

Tonight I returned to the primary school for the Ryedale Roadshow – the local comprehensive was doing a tour of the local primaries. While the world teetered on the brink of another war in the Gulf and reeled from yet more atrocities in the Balkans, senior staff reassured anxious parents and their children about such perplexing subjects as school lunches, buses and uniforms. The presentation was upbeat and very modern, complete with a PowerPoint presentation, or what would have been a PowerPoint presentation had the projector worked. Paul, the Head of Lower School, who was leading the presentation, was unfazed and went into a positively Dr Strangelove mode, pointing out things on the blank screen which blatantly weren't there. 'To the left of the new ICT room you will see the gym and as we enter, notice the climbing wall on the left, being scaled by Will Johnson, the Edmund Hillary of the Vale of Pickering. Then along the covered walkway to the main hall, where Rev'd Wilbourne is leading assembly and regaling us with yet another of his jokes: "Knock, knock," says the Rev. "Who's there?" says the Head. "John," replies the Rev. "John who?" asks the Head. "John the Baptist," the Rev concludes, emptying a glass of water over the Head's head.' Paul, as well as being Head of Lower School, was also Head of Drama, hence his talent for improvisation. Chatting to him afterwards, I mentioned Laura's debut in *The Sound of Music* earlier in the day. He amazed me with a lengthy in-depth analysis of how *The Sound of Music* had more parallels with Shakespeare's *Romeo and Juliet* than *Westside Story*. It wasn't the sort of conversation one normally has in a primary school, but I was captivated as Paul explained with great animation how Captain and Maria von Trapp's flight from Austria to America was equivalent to the star-crossed lovers' suicide in Shakespeare's original. It all took me back to my schooldays, where teachers were resources of encyclopaedic quality for their particular subject, their enthusiasm contagious, setting you up for a lifetime. I recall my old history teacher talking about the Tudors as if he had been to college with Henry VIII! As an educational practitioner, he probably would have left a lot to be desired, but as a resource for a lifetime he was brilliant. In these days where educational practice seems the be-all and end-all, it was good to see my old history teacher's spirit was still alive in men such as Paul.

🖤 *Ash Wednesday, 25th February*

Today was a nightmare, in that a heavy shower dowsed the wonderful bonfire of palm crosses I had got going outside the vestry door – the custom is to burn the remnant of last year's palm crosses to make the ash for tonight's service of penitence. I had no other recourse than to draft in charcoal we normally use to make incense, using that to make the mark of the cross on the foreheads of the forty or so souls who turned up to be ashed. It was only after employing the charcoal liberally that I realised it was self-igniting. I only hoped none of my congregation would go near a naked flame for a while, otherwise they would be returning to the dust from which they came a little sooner than any of us had anticipated. Of particular concern was my patron, Lord Feversham, who sports a pipe and on whose noble head I had chalked the biggest cross of them all.

He faithfully comes to the altar rail, week by week, humbly the last to receive, wincing slightly as he kneels down – 'It's not you I'm wincing at, Vicar, it's the gout,' were the words uttered by my Lord before receiving the Lord. He winced as usual tonight – was it the gout, or was it anticipating that he might go up like a Roman Candle because of this stupid boy of a vicar?

🍃 *Friday, 27th February*

During the Second World War, Leslie Newman, a Methodist minister, rode around Yorkshire on horseback, following in John Wesley's steps (or rather hooves). Reading his account spurred me on to try the same trick – though by bike rather than horse. Last Saturday I began by cycling 25 miles south, through a Castle Howard haunted by Sydney Smith. Smith, an early nineteenth-century English cleric, wit and editor of the *Edinburgh Review*, surprisingly had a parish in these parts, often dining with the Carlisles at Castle Howard. I say surprisingly because of his comment, 'I have no relish for the country. It is a kind of unholy grave!' Despite this he remained as vicar of nearby Foston for twenty years, rebuilding the ruin of a vicarage and farming the 300 acres of glebe land, dazzling a far wider audience than his rustic congregation with his characteristically acerbic wit, best exemplified by his comment about his old enemy, the Bishop of Exeter: 'I must believe in the Apostolic Succession, there being no other way of accounting for the descent of the Bishop of Exeter from Judas Iscariot.'

Chuckling at these and other Sydney Smithisms was the best distraction therapy from the sharp muscle pain in my legs, caused by cycling up too many hills. Eventually I reached the Yorkshire Wolds and their gorgeous little churches, each perched on a characteristically rounded hilltop within sight of the other. I lunched in the ruins of Kirkham Abbey, nestling by the River Derwent as it bisects Yorkshire on its journey from Scarborough to the Humber. In a sense it was like coming home, in that in the twelfth century Kirkham's Augustinian canons had travelled to Helmsley and built the church there, calling their hastily constructed and temporary lodging Canons Garth (literally, Garden for the Canons). Despite my return visit just eight centuries later, the site's English Heritage attendant was very suspicious of my bicycle, which I propped up against his booth. He examined it thoroughly with a serious face 'to make sure it's not a terrorist bomb'. They must have had a lot of trouble with exploding bicycles at shy little Kirkham.

Since neither I nor my bike exploded last Saturday, today I decided to venture further afield and cycled to Wensleydale, 45 miles to Helmsley's west. The 8-mile climb out of Helmsley to Sutton Bank took its toll, and I paused at the top for a Mars bar and apple juice, taking great gulps of freezing air into my lungs as I sat on a bench and looked at the Vale of York and Vale of Mowbray spread out before my gaze. It all looked so lush and green, in marked contrast to the top of the Bank, which was covered by a foot of snow, making my shoes sodden for the rest of the journey.

Despite the sodden shoes, cycling down Sutton Bank to Sutton under Whitestonecliff, dropping 3000 yards in two-thirds of a mile, was sheer white-knuckle-ride thrill. I had a flashback to a conversation I had had recently with a sheep-farmer's wife, who recalled how in the war, she had belonged to a group of young farm lads and their lasses who regularly cycled this route of a summer's evening, to go to the flicks in Thirsk. 'I was a bit cautious on t' bike, Vicar. Jim, my young man was always racing ahead of me and then had to wait for me to catch up,' my farmer's wife explained. 'One night he reached the Bank's bottom at breakneck pace and let the rest of the group go ahead as he waited for me – I was lagging behind as usual. But when I failed to appear, t' silly bugger assumed I'd changed my mind and gone home, so cycled on to t' cinema alone. Not that he was alone for long. I heard he spent the film snogging Maisie Smith in the back row; that trollop was anybody's for a smoke and a bag of pop-corn.'

'So why did you turn around?' I asked.

'I didn't turn around,' she replied crossly, 'I'd braked too harshly on one of them hairpin bends and had gone head over heels over t' handlebars. Fortunately I 'ad a softish landing in a gorse bush, but was stuck in its briars for over an hour until some airmen from t' air base at t' top o' Bank spotted me, came to me rescue and drove me and my buckled bike safely home.' The farmer's wife paused for a breath and began to blush. 'I was so embarrassed, Vicar. My summer dress was flimsy enough to begin with and had been torn to shreds by that gorse. Those airmen couldn't take their eyes off me for the whole journey. Or their hands, come to that!'

She had a far away look in her eyes, and in sharp contrast to the fierce frown she had nursed for our conversation up until now (a frown which would have done Nora Batty proud), the faintest of smiles crossed her lips. Come to think of it, I wasn't too sure whether she was blushing or whether a rosy glow had come over her.

'I guess you finished with your young man for abandoning you,' I commented, anxious to move the conversation on from any further revelations.

'Oh no, Vicar, I married him. I've made him pay these past fifty years, believe you me. There's never a day goes by when I don't remind him of that night!'

Back to today, coming up to the Bank's top, every revolution of the pedals had been a torment; now they whizzed around freely, at the greatest of speed, like an airplane propeller. The problem was that afterwards my over-heated pedal-crank bearings kept seizing up, so every few miles I had to enlist mechanical assistance to free up things. By the end of the journey I had called at two farms, two garages and one combine harvester centre and all cheerfully came to my assistance. At the latter, a mechanic broke into his lunch hour to send me on my way; at a farm the farmer's wife let me rummage in the boot of her husband's car, expensive golf clubs hurled aside as we sought a socket set. Sans dog collar; just decked with cycle helmet and mud-splattered cagoule, I would look a shambles. And yet people helped and trusted me without question, never once suspecting my bike was of the exploding kind.

🍂 Saturday, 28th February

Having reached Wensleydale by dusk last night, this morning I climbed out of the dale to overlook Swaledale. James Herriot always maintained that the view from the Wensleydale–Swaledale pass overlooking tiny Reeth was the best view in the world, and he was spot on. The steep dale sides, criss-crossed with dry stone walls, the farm houses precariously perched on the hillsides, the silver River Swale winding through the narrow dale was the most gorgeous of sights. It was such a clear day that I could make out a tiny York Minster as well as the cooling towers of the Tees and Humber and Drax, belching boundary markers for the York Diocese. I silently held that diocese in one privileged gaze; there wasn't even a voice whispering, 'All this I will give you if you but fall down and worship me.'

At least not until I headed back to Helmsley, my pedal crank clunking on every revolution. It wasn't Satan tempting me, simply my brain reminding me it was the First Sunday in Lent tomorrow, with the temptations of Jesus looming large in the Gospel reading for the day. I had already preached on that very Gospel for the previous sixteen First Sundays in Lent, spanning my entire ministry; what could I say that was fresh? 'Take it easy on yourself, use one of your old sermons,' a voice whispered. 'No, write something new,' another voice counselled, 'they might not have heard it, but you have. We can't have you being bored by your own sermons!'

And so I composed something new, if a little crazy, touching on wronged lovers hurtling over handlebars and helpful combine harvester mechanics and not hearing strange voices on the brink of Swaledale.

🍃 *Sunday, 1st March*

In Lent we're staging *Helmsley's Biggest Read*, where parishioners have voted for their favourite biblical book, with special talks on the top five at Lenten evensongs, followed by a final vote for Helmsley's Top of the Biblical Pops. It's all part of a cunning plan to get folk back to church, to seduce them into giving up giving up Evening Prayer for Lent.

The reasons for opting for a particular biblical book touch the heart. For instance, one doctor's wife nominated St Luke's Gospel because in the 1960s her mother-in-law suffered the severest of strokes which twisted her body, confining her to bed for the final two years of her life. Throughout that time son and daughter-in-law nursed and fed her, their knees wearing the bedside rug threadbare as they knelt to minister to her. Each evening the daughter-in-law read her mother-in-law a chapter from Luke's Gospel, her favourite book of the Bible – over the two years they read the whole Gospel together three times, poring repeatedly over certain well-loved passages. The Gospel clearly soaked into the old lady's soul. 'What's today's date?' a visiting medic asked, suspicious of her state of mind. 'Why, it's Ascension Day,' came her Lucan reply, fazing the GP who had thought it was just another Thursday. Her Nunc Dimittis coincided with the Tuesday of Holy Week, a very Lucan time to die.

And then there's the moors sheep farmer, 87 years young, who chants the Psalms as he tramps the hills. Local ewes have an annoying habit of saving the most difficult of births for the middle of the wintriest of nights. There's something supremely poignant about this old chap, wrapped in the thinnest of coats, reciting Psalm 8 and Psalm 104 to while away the long night hours, the one man left awake, watching his flocks in company with the bleary-eyed God of David.

Speaking of my namesake, the tiniest of 9-year-olds nominated I Samuel, because it was the book which featured the battle of all battles with Goliath. 'Though David is only small, he kills a giant,' the little lad explained, as if I had never come across the tale before. His choice touched me, as I imagined him heartened by the story as manifold playground Goliaths stamped on him, firmly believing that one day his stone would come.

Of course, being called David myself, I had come across the story before. The grey tedium of my childhood, compounded by the paucity of toys and books, was relieved by the sixteen colour pictures in my King James Bible, which I used to pore over. True to form, there was massive Goliath and a diminutive David, with cheeks so rosy it looked as if the artist had overdone the rouge. The Old Testament ended curiously with a picture of Absalom, caught by his hair in the boughs of an oak tree, with his mule racing off over the horizon. Keen to glean a moral from all biblical tales, I resolved that when I became an adult I would keep my hair short and steer my ass clear of sprawling oak trees.

Once I could read, I found Absalom's story marvellously bewildering. Such as when he stages his coup and mounts a tent on the roof of his father's palace and (in the quaint euphemism of the King James Bible) goes into ten of his father David's concubines, in front of the whole host of Israel. All the roofs I knew were steeply pitched and made of slate tiles, invariably wet, so I imagined Absalom slithering and slipping and holding on for dear life as he went from one concubine to another. In my innocence I guessed a concubine was a sort of porcupine. In those benighted days, Pathe News footage of Queen Elizabeth's coronation, with Michael Ramsey swaying beside her, punctuated every cinema visit. To my infant imagination Absalom's coronation seemed so much more exciting. Ten porcupines!

🍂 *Tuesday, 10th March*

A vicarage is like a planet with a very powerful gravitational pull, and you need a massive escape velocity to free yourself from its clutches. You'll be setting off in good time for an appointment, but the phone will ring or there'll be a knock on the door. You always think, 'This'll only take a minute,' but invariably it's a complex matter that takes ages and you find you are hopelessly late yet again.

That was the situation this morning as I left Canons Garth at the precise time I should have been arriving at Ryedale School. I pedalled furiously the three or so miles, deciding to leave the main road and take a short cut up the ominously named Rape Lane. Going downhill with the wind behind me, I must have been exceeding 25 mph when a large hare appeared just a few feet in front of me, out of nowhere. It stood its ground in the middle of the road as I hurtled towards it, applying my brakes but preparing myself for the inevitable collision. In the seconds before impact I imagined myself being thrown over the handle-bars; I imagined the hare, the most beautiful of creatures, being fatally wounded as my bike smashed into her. But no collision happened. Just a millisecond before impact the hare leapt the leap of all leaps, clearing my head by inches, a veritable hare's breadth! When I was a boy my pet sheepdog used to chase the hares that surrounded our country vicarage. Like any sheepdog, she was fast, but the hares always outran and outmanoeuvred her. Ever since, I have had the greatest admiration for these fleetest of animals, that admiration doubled today as I stopped my bike and watched in sheer homage as the hare darted across the fields and within a few seconds was just a speck on the horizon.

The lane rose through a dense wood above the school, where my path was blocked by some lumberjacks felling pine. I carried my bike over several large trunks that had fallen across the road, ignored by the hard-hatted tree fellers, who seemed oblivious to the fact that they were obstructing the traffic, or at least obstructing one vicar, already late for his appointment. Having completed the assault course, I remounted my bike, but as I gained speed I realised that the clasp must have come undone on my briefcase clipped above the rear wheel, with confidential papers billowing out in all directions. I dismounted once again and managed to retrieve all of them from the hedgerows and ditches, and crammed them, muddy but intact, back into my case, as I set off once again for the final 200 yards, praying for no more delays.

As it was I arrived at the school 20 minutes late, with the Head hovering anxiously by the main door. 'Don't worry, David, you're not the last. One of the candidates has been held up in traffic on the ring road.' A few weeks before I had been elected Chair of Governors, quite a coup for a new boy, and this was my first time chairing an interview board for a couple of teaching posts. Arriving late, hair windswept, my clothes and my papers muddied wasn't quite the epitome of professionalism that I was trying to convey, but never mind, at least I was here.

The candidate who was even later than me arrived, and the interviews began. I kicked off with the first question, an easy-peasy one, drawn from the detail on the candidates' own application forms to set them at their ease. One candidate had listed aromatherapy as her hobby, so I asked her what smell she would pump through the classroom to sharpen the pupils' mental abilities. She looked nonplussed, as if the idea that smell could sharpen the senses had never ever crossed her mind. At the same time she gave me the oddest of looks – she clearly thought someone had kidnapped the chair of governors and replaced him with a madman. 'You did list aromatherapy as your hobby,' I said, trying to redeem myself from being certifiable.

'Did I really?' she replied incredulously. After a painful pause of several seconds, she piped up with 'Peppermint,' before lapsing into a further long silence. I passed her on to the Deputy Head who asked her a more sensible question about how to discipline a Year 9 lad who was doing something unmentionable beneath a desk.

Uncowed, I noticed the next candidate had mentioned in his papers that he had a terrific sense of humour. Lest he had forgotten, I reminded him of this before asking him to tell us a joke or describe a funny incident he had witnessed. Again the lengthy silence before the flattest of responses, 'Sorry, I can't think of anything funny.' Hardly the comedian of the year, then.

You could tell the next candidate was the one we were going to appoint as soon as he walked into the room, confident, personable, humorous and professional, a born educator and entertainer. And male. Not that we were chauvinist or misogynist, but we were looking for a French teacher, and this was rural North Yorkshire. The thing is, memories go back a long way in these parts, and in 1069 William the Conqueror, as part of his conquest of Britain, harried the North, burning its villages and crops and even salting the ground, dictating famine for a century. The locals, particularly the lads, have never forgotten or forgiven it, and are resistant to anything that smacks of Normandy or French. So we have to make sure that any French teachers are macho and confident; pumping pep-permint through the classrooms or failing to tell a single joke just would not wash.

Interestingly, although just fifty years back the Germans all but flattened Hull and bombed Middlesbrough, York and even the moors, we have no problem with pupils taking German, whose guttural sounds speak to the guttural Viking sounds lurking behind every local place name, and no doubt in every local gene. But French is clearly the language of the oppressor, to be resisted at all costs.

Having been fortified with a fish and chip lunch, far, far better than the horsemeat and mashed potato infused with dinner ladies' hair of my schooldays, we embarked on the afternoon's interviews for a Maths post. I changed tack, ignored what the candidates had written in their papers, and simply asked them to describe their best ever lesson. One chap spent a tedious twenty minutes describing how he had sexed up Pythagoras' theorem. By the end of which I and the Deputy, both mathematicians, nursed that same puzzled look, wonder-ing whether the Pythagoras' theorem this bloke was dribbling on about was different from the one we both knew and loved, namely that the square on a triangle's hypotenuse was equal to the sum of the squares of the other two sides. If this was this guy's best shot, then no wonder kids found Maths so hard to grasp. Needless to say, he didn't get the job.

I was taught Maths by one of the funniest men I have ever encountered, who made a joke out of every theorem. We could hardly wait for the next Maths lesson, with the anticipation of witnessing a stand-up's latest routine. We remembered the jokes, bandied them around, and because of that remembered the theorems. Ever since I have firmly believed that humour is the greatest of teaching aids, not just for Maths but also for Christianity.

Saturday, 21st March

The tiniest of 9-year-olds goggled with the rest of my confirmation class at the sheer size of the angel towering above them. 'Its wings are moving,' one of them shrieked. No, we weren't indulging in some corporate mystical experience, but were simply visiting Gateshead on the first leg of our church outing. At the closest of range, we admired the girders of the magnificent Angel of the North, opened only last month, but the girders already rusting. Every child just had to have a photo taken of themselves, dwarfed by angelic feet. I flashed back to a visit Archbishop John Habgood made to Russia in pre-Glasnost days, a tour where they were guided throughout by their Marxist interpreter and minder. She clearly pitied these silly Westerners, naively clinging to a superstitious faith which sensible Russian citizens had long since grown out of. However, in Leningrad they encountered a massive angelic statue. 'Gentlemen,' she lectured in her broken English, 'here you see a life-sized statue of an angel!' An atheist, yet privy to angelic dimensions.

The next stop on our confirmation roadshow was the Northumberland coast opposite Lindisfarne, where we abandoned our coach to walk three miles across the causeway to Holy Island. Fortunately our trip was sufficiently well planned to coincide with low tide, so I had foolishly expected something akin to a pleasant stroll along the beach on a sunny first day of spring. Instead we squelched through the blackest of mud, slithered across the slimiest of seaweed, and waded through channels of water, deep yet fortunately surprisingly warm for Northumberland. It was a true pilgrimage, literally with a baptism flavour, reminiscent of the Israelites crossing the Red Sea, although Psalm 66's author, in waxing lyrical about God turning the sea into dry land, was clearly a clueless landlubber. I guess the reality was similar to what we were experiencing, and I imagined the moans of the sodden Israelites: 'You never told us it was going to be this muddy ... Aagh, I've got some sea-weed stuck between my toes ... I wish I'd stayed on the coach ... Moses, why didn't you tell me to bring Wellingtons?'

Eventually we reached the dry shore of Lindisfarne, where we visited the abbey and sat and ate our well-deserved picnics while we endured a frightfully cheerful church group from Tyneside trilling, 'Give me joy in my heart!' I am a priest and a child of the vicarage, thoroughly immersed in church life, yet why is it I always want to strangle people who flaunt their faith? We walked around the castle, peered into the lime kilns, scrambled out to a headland bleached by salty winds, and then breathlessly boarded our coach to return to the mainland, just an hour before the fateful spring high tide was due.

At which point disaster struck. The bus was of the high-tech variety, with a clever suspension which lowered its front so that passengers could hop on and hop off without performing a leap of Olympic standards. The problem was that, once we were all on board, the suspension wouldn't raise the vehicle back up again. The driver gamely tried to move the vehicle anyway, but its front gorged out pieces of tarmac like an ice-cream scoop.

Fortunately the driver doubled up (literally) as a mechanic, and for 45 anxious minutes he tried to coax the suspension to operate. 'This is a modern bus, and it kneels when stationary,' his wife reassured us, 'the problem is it just won't stop kneeling.' But suddenly the bus rose up, like an ox rousing itself from its sleep, and we sped back to the mainland across the causeway, the

imminent high tide lapping our tyres. We were too busy to
kneel on Holy Island, but our bus did, in sheer homage
to St Aidan and the forlorn headquarters he chose to bring
Christianity to a gloomy North.

🐚 *Wednesday, 25th March*

I always like a confirmation to have special features which will
stay with the candidates for ever. We started tonight's confirmation in total darkness, the candidates processing in from the font
holding candles, bringing light to cheer the church. We try to
cheer up one of the dark transept chapels where Vicar Gray
installed the black marble altar by having a votive candle stand
before a statue of a Madonna and Child. Tonight we had moved
the candle stand and statue into the centre of the church, and
having processed in, the candidates put their candles on the
stand, symbolically bringing their light to Jesus, the source of all
light. Tonight is the feast of the Annunciation, so it was good to
have a statue of Mary on centre stage, her yes to God's call
juxtaposed with the candidates' yes.

Taking up the Madonna and child theme, the 14 youngsters
were presented to the Bishop by their mothers, who had
nurtured them from conception and baptism and were now
passing them on to Christian adulthood. As each mother boldly
and bravely said 'My Lord Bishop, I present my child N to be
confirmed,' I could hardly hold back the tears. Rowan Williams, my tutor at theological college, had told us that if ever we
feared we were about to break down in a public service, we
should offset the tears by thinking about a funny thing that had
happened to us.

I thought back to our Shrove Tuesday party for the confirmation candidates, when we got to talking about the subject of

loss, which for most children focuses on the death of pets. My sympathetic cooing about someone's hamster dying was interrupted by one lad declaring,

'My dad's a duck murderer!'

'Oh, I'm sorry,' I replied, 'so he killed them for food?'

'No, when he'd killed 'em he chucked 'em in bin!'

'When was this?' I asked assuming the event was recent.

'It were three years ago, and he murdered four of 'em. He crept up behind them and tapped 'em on 'ead with his stick. And what's more, they were mi pets, they were named ducks!' he continued, doubly affronted. 'One of them was even called Charles,' he concluded, grinning at Charles, another confirmation candidate. Charles turned pale at the prospect of being tapped on the head and declined his eighth pancake. It was a funny little incident, and thinking about it kept the tears at bay. Rowan's advice had clearly worked.

I thought back to 1992, when I told my then boss, Archbishop Habgood, that Rowan had been elected as Bishop of Monmouth. John Habgood, who very rarely lost his temper, was furious. 'But we need someone of his calibre to stay at Oxford, fight the Church of England's corner amongst all those academics. What on earth does he want to go to a backwater like South Wales for and play at toy church?' I kept silence, after all, Archbishop's chaplains, like Victorian children, should be seen and not heard. But privately I felt my boss was being more than a little harsh. Knowing Rowan as I did, I sensed that going to South Wales would be his beginning rather than his end. And any church is a toy church, playing at heaven, in the sense that a critical element of children's play, playing mummies and daddies, doctors and nurses, is rehearsing in their imagination for a certain future. And if South Wales was a backwater, then it had got something in common with another backwater called Nazareth.

Besides, we had two very good friends in Cardiff, whose wedding we'd been to a few years back. Inevitably at the reception we found ourselves seated with the local clergy. They proved the jolliest bunch, in stark contrast to some Church of England gatherings that sometimes could have the darkness of a Shakespearean tragedy about them. I learnt later that John Habgood had had his eye on Rowan to be the next Bishop of Durham, so was understandably miffed that somewhere else had snapped him up, as piqued as someone who saw the love of his life marrying another.

Saturday, 28th March

A night out with the girls to the Helmsley Arts Theatre and Cinema to watch the latest Bond film, *Tomorrow Never Dies*. Whenever we attend our small cinema at Helmsley, invariably the only seats available are on the front row. I just have to hope my upfront presence doesn't spoil the audience's enjoyment – a priest and some of James Bond's risqué words and actions can make uneasy cinema-fellows. I sympathise with Pope John XXIII, who was at a party also attended by a youthful Sophia Loren, sporting the most revealing of low-cut dresses. Inevitably someone asked the Pope whether he thought her attire appropriate. 'I feel so sorry for her husband,' he confessed. 'With such a beautiful wife, when she made her entrance all eyes in the room should have been on her. But instead they were all on me!'

Sunday, 29th March

Ruth looks like winning Helmsley's Biggest Read, with parishioners voting for their favourite biblical book following my erudite(ish) lectures at Lenten evensongs. It's probably because when I preached on Ruth, I juxtaposed her with a Holocaust Testimonial recently sent to us by an Israeli friend. Both Ruth and the Testimonial involved Jews and Gentiles, asylum seekers and people in flight, tyrannies and constant threats, all seasoned with a certain cunning.

Our friend Pessy was two when she and her parents were hidden in a tiny cupboard by kindly Gentile neighbours, when Stormtroopers rounded up the Jews on Kristallnacht 1938. Her family's rapid flight across Europe then followed the direction of the arrows in the opening sequence of *Dad's Army*, ending up stranded on the Dunkirk beaches. Pessy's mother approached a British captain. 'Take us with you,' she begged.

'Madam, it is simply not possible,' he replied. 'The troops are already packed like sardines onto the boats; there's not enough room for them, let alone you civilians.'

Then the captain was relieved by another, and Pessy's mother tried again. 'Take us with you,' she begged.

'Madam, it is simply not possible,' came the same chilling reply. 'We have to give priority to our British soldiers.'

Quick as a flash Pessy's mother snatched the gun from his belt and held it desperately to her little girl's head. 'If you don't take us, I'll shoot my daughter, my husband and myself. We'd be better off dead than butchered by the Nazis.'

I quote from Pessy's account: 'He took fright and said, "Come on then, Madam, come quickly." I remember how he pushed us into a boat, a tiny boat. Mercifully, I don't remember the gun.'

But once in England, their troubles were far from over. German-speaking with no papers, they were initially interned as enemy aliens. Once cleared, there was an endless trudge around a London suburb looking for lodgings, with 'No Jews here' the order of the day. Finally a Gentile couple rented them an attic, her father found work and with his first week's wage bought a pair of candlesticks so that his little family, with nothing except their precious freedom, could keep their Sabbath.

I've quoted only a small section of a very raw Ruth-like account, with the incident at Dunkirk surely a macabre acting out of 'Where you die, I will die ...' My only suspicion is that parishioners aren't actually voting for the book of Ruth; they're really voting for the book of Pessy.

🍂 Palm Sunday, 5th April

During my ministry, I've encouraged many people to be Jesus, to play the part of Jesus in the Passion Gospel read in full today. I've gone for the conventional choice, a retired priest, severely afflicted with church-voice-itis, who made Jesus sound so very, very churchy, like a posh announcer on the BBC's Home Service: 'Truuly, I tell yooo, today yooo will be with me in paradise.'

But more often than not, I've gone for the unconventional choice, even sought my Jesuses from outside the church family, and have been surprised and heartened.

I recall a consultant neurologist, whose skill as a brain surgeon had rescued so many people, brought so many people back from the brink. He told me how once he had sat up through the night with his toddler grandson. The toddler had banged his head, as toddlers are wont to do: 'He'll be fine,' the GP had said. But his grandfather had sat up beside his cot through the night, watching for signs, signs of life, signs of death.

He made me think of God the Father watching each and every one of us through our dark nights, desiring life, willing life in all its fullness. He made me think of God the Father watching his son through his dark night, watching him die. He played Jesus very straight, a very humble, quiet voice: 'Father, into your hands I commend my spirit.'

I once asked our GP to be Jesus, an unusual doctor who sought healing for his patients by encouraging them to join his poetry group. Poetry on the NHS! This poetic doctor, who had seen many births and many deaths, was strangely moved and moving when he acted the part of this ultimate death. As soon as Jesus died his bleeper went off and he rushed out to attend an urgent case.

Another time I asked the local butcher to be Jesus, which shocked my middle-class congregation no end. I've spent a lot of my time hanging around butchers' shops, I like talking to butchers who always seem to have a wisdom of their own. We have a lot in common. They feed the world with meat while I feed the world with Christ. John's Gospel has Christ dying at the very moment that the Passover lambs are being sacrificed in the temple. My butcher friend would have seen a lot of lambs die. I felt he was well qualified to play the Lamb of God in his final fatal hours. He played him beautifully, again softly spoken, with his natural Yorkshire inflections, 'My God, my God, why hast thou forsaken me?'

We had the village carpenter play Jesus in my first parish. He took a break from carving his replacement windows and dining-room furniture to carve himself an imaginary cross and be crucified before our eyes. His Jesus was so gentle, so tender, as if he was sawing, planing, sanding, carefully carving death itself, unfolding it before our eyes, as if it was his greatest work, no longer a thing to be feared.

Shockingly I have asked two women to play Jesus. When a cathedral in New York featured a woman, Christa, on the cross, people were outraged, as if crucifixion only happened to men. One of my female Jesuses was a lawyer. In the Gospels lawyers attack Jesus at every turn. This Palm Sunday we bucked the trend because a lawyer was Him, a young mother, blonde, Aryan, a joyful Jesus even unto death.

The other woman is a Christ figure if ever there was one, and she played Jesus for us at our service today, a German teacher at our local school, her mother a Christian, her father a Hindu. She proved as brilliant at being Jesus as she is at being a teacher, always reconciling, soothing, healing, a veritable angel caring for colleagues and pupils alike.

Ryedale School have been hosting a group from Germany on exchange at the school, and so I got them to act the other parts. The German physics teacher carried off Judas rather well, with his 'Ze one I shall kiss iz der man! Seize him and lead him away safely!' A little girl who was a Russian German brought tears to my eyes and her voice will haunt me until the day I die: she read the part of the crowd on Palm Sunday with her plaintiff cry, 'Hosianna, Hosianna, blessings on him who comes in the name of the Lord.' There was a pathos there of Mother Russia intensity which opened a chill door and let Good Friday in on Palm Sunday.

Another year we had a newly qualified English teacher, a young man whom all the Year 10 girls fancied. His Jesus was very fast, very urgent, like a crucial lesson that needed delivering as soon as possible for the salvation of all his pupils.

And the best Jesus? Well, they've all been brilliant, all made me see things in Jesus which I had never realised before. But of the two that really stay in my memory, one was an atheist. He was deputy head at our local comp and he was the ultimate fixer. A Year 8 Geography class were once discussing a recent earthquake, which had devastated a whole region. 'What do people need there to recover?' the teacher asked, thinking of temporary shelters and water tankers and food and financial aid. One child hesitantly put her hand up and said, 'Please, Miss, they need our deputy head!' I don't think a single member of the class, including the teacher, thought for one moment that

that deputy wouldn't be able to put everything straight. Whatever anyone asked him to do, he would sort and sort well. So I
asked him to be Christ.

Despite being an atheist, he was a simply wonderful Christ,
softly spoken, every word was heartfelt. 'Father, forgive them,
for they know not what they do.' Archbishop Michael Ramsey
always believed that he would meet atheists in heaven. I'm sure I
will meet that deputy. I've always felt that an atheist was
someone whom God hadn't discovered yet. Or maybe God's
closer to them than we believers realise, we who keep God at a
safe impassionate distance. Certainly he delivered Jesus straight,
freed up from all the trappings and clutter which can make us
religious folk so easily miss him.

The other Jesus is my first one. When I was a curate in
Middlesbrough I took my wife Rachel a cup of tea in bed at
8am on Palm Sunday. As I drank my tea, I came up with an idea.
'Let's act out the Gospel,' I said. 'You can be the narrator, I'll be
the other voices and we'll get David to be Jesus.' The service
where we were going to do all this was at 9am!

David was my fellow curate and as I was getting dressed I
gave him a ring. No answer! 'I'm sure he's there,' I said to
Rachel. 'You go across to church and tell them I'm coming and
I'll drive over to his house.' His house was only a mile or so
away, the curtains still drawn as I rapped on the door. Eventually
David opened his bedroom window and stuck his bedraggled
head out. 'What do you want?' he sleepily said.

'David, I want you to be Jesus at the 9am Communion,' I
shouted. Goodness knows what his neighbours thought.

'OK,' he replied, 'I'll just get washed and dressed and try to
join you in time.' I drove off, robed, began the communion on
the look out for David as we sang *All Glory Laud and Honour* and
the *Kyries* and said the collect. The Lesson reader took his time,
thank God, and for the first and only time in my life I tried to
slow the Gradual Hymn down, when my normal practice is to
speed sullen hymns up.

We began the Gospel and on cue David walked in. We hadn't rehearsed, we only had the small print of the Alternative Service Book in front of us, our parts unmarked. It would have been so easy to make a slip, read the wrong part, make the Passion into a farce. Yet we didn't. It all went just fine, beautifully, as if God was carrying our one-take. Maybe Jesus doesn't brook too much rehearsal, better when he comes upon us all of a sudden, with his 'Leave all that and follow me!'

Holy Week and its story contains an invitation. Not to see this as a story that happened two thousand years ago in a distant land, but to stage it now in our own world, our own context, our own families. Even to dare to be Jesus ourselves, to bring all that we are to the part of Jesus and to bring all that Jesus was and is to colour our part in life, and let it be none other than life-changing; death-changing.

Back to Middlesbrough, David's voice was just right, not churchy, rather it was real, tender, drawing you into the Passion, the love that went unto death. I soon left Middlesbrough; David stayed, working in various Urban Priority Area parishes. No longer well, he is mostly housebound. I guess it won't be long before there comes another surprise knock on his door early one morning. Not me this time, but the Christ he played so beautifully way back in 1984 come to call him home. My first Jesus and the very best.

🍂 *Holy Monday, 6th April*

Way back in February I planned a dawn Eucharist for Monday in Holy Week in Rievaulx Abbey. From my wintry study, I imagined a balmy spring April morning, with my congregation warmed by the rising sun, glad that they were not in Helmsley now a-bed. It didn't quite turn out as I'd hoped. I crept away from home at 6.15am in a blizzard and cycled into a Rievaulx carpeted with snow. I opened my rucksack and took out my kit: the tiny silver chalice and paten, the picnic flasks containing water and wine, the crumpled purificator and corporal, the battered Prayer Book, the priest's wafer, already broken. I set them out on a chipped stone altar in a chantry chapel, covered by no cloth of crisp, white, starched linen: just a cloth of snow. By the end of communion, the warm leather of the prayer book had thawed a watery rectangle, the chalice and paten had each thawed its own circle. Afterwards I cycled up the steepest of banks, climbed over the locked gate into the Rievaulx Terraces and looked down upon the abbey from my lofty perch. I could make out the footprints of my small congregation, the thawed-out green patches where they had shivered for communion, the circles and rectangle on the altar. I love the countryside when it is covered in snow, gazing in homage at the tracks left by the invisible animals of the night. That Holy Week dawn we had left our own tracks; or had God left his?

◗ Holy Wednesday, 8th April

I do sympathise with churches agonising over whether to be locked or unlocked. The price of keeping our church open here is the occasional act of vandalism – we suffered a particularly vicious attack today and had to clean up by night to restore the place in time for Maundy Thursday's dawn. The almsboxes have been ransacked yet again. Though there are volunteers who act as guard and guide, it proves impossible to man the church all the time. And an open but deserted church has its own quality, with the absence of hale and hearty greetings allowing the quiet prayerfulness of the place to seep in.

But at a price. This time even the moneybox on the votive candle stand has been wrenched open with candles scattered and the votive candle stand mangled. Nearby is the intercessions book, thrown on the floor by the thief, containing the heartfelt pleas of folk carrying so much tragedy: for a child orphaned when his parents died at sea; for a daughter and son-in-law coming to terms with the still-birth of their first child; for a marriage on the rocks ... Such prayers the thief has so meanly desecrated.

The words of St Patrick's Breastplate well up inside me, as I sit before the wounded stand. Some years back I was bored with watching the video, *Four Weddings and a Funeral*, so I stole into the kitchen and learnt the ten-verse hymn off by heart, as you do. Now I chant it as a sort of re-hallowing, railing 'against the hostile men that mar my course. Or few or many, far or nigh, in every place, and in all hours, against their fierce hostility, I bind to me these holy powers.'

Modern hymnologists omit these 'cursing verses', sneering at their thinly disguised form of white magic. I recall when I first encountered them, during a choir practice at Westcott House a couple of decades ago, led by the ubiquitous Rowan Williams in a shadowy set straight from *Death in Holy Orders*. 'These verses are primitive and dark,' Rowan commented, 'and should probably be best left out.' But then he added, 'Oh go on, let's leave them in,' giving a naughty-but-nice sort of smile.

A later line warns of 'the knowledge that defiles'. 'Dr Williams, what's that?' one unctuous student enquired. 'I'm not going to tell you,' Rowan beamed gnostically. Then I seem to recall a shiver, as a door opened into a chill future when it wouldn't just be ordinands Rowan would have to shield from the knowledge that defiles.

Maundy Thursday, 9th April

Derek, my head server, having heard about the break-in, last night dropped in to offer help. He picked up the mangled stand

and bundled it into his car, with a simple, 'I'll see what I can do.' This morning the stand is returned, straightened out, repainted, a new lid welded on the moneybox, this time with a double padlock fitted. Derek must have worked the entire night through to make it better than new. Maundy Thursday traditionally is a day of dark deeds: Judas' betrayal, Peter's denial, all the disciples forsaking Jesus and fleeing. It's really touching when someone bucks that dark trend with a sacrificial act of sheer devotion such as Derek's.

Derek is one of those rare guys you could never tire of spending all day with. Before retirement he was a postman, mostly delivering on the moors. The van would drop him off with his heavy sack in a morning, and he would walk the route, mile after mile up and down the steep hills and valleys, in all weathers. He didn't just deliver the mail, but checked up on folk in their remote farms and cottages, having a chat and a laugh with them, sharing a welcome cuppa. Once he was accompanied by a fiercely efficient time-and-motion man from the head office at York, who was puzzled by the coincidence that the kettle was always boiling in each and every isolated home at the precise moment of their visit. But that morning no one let on about the pastoral side to Derek the postman's job, and by the end of the most gruelling of 16-mile walks, the time-and-motion man felt Derek earned every penny.

Derek was also a skilled mechanic, with a mend-it rather than replace-it approach. He had purchased an Austin Seven which had been abandoned in someone's barn, rusting and rotting. Now the Austin Seven, like our votive stand, was better than new. Derek displayed it at church events such as garden parties and fayres and always had a queue of admirers who often stood speechless, in homage at the car and the restorer's skill. Not only did Derek buck the dark trend of Maundy Thursday; he was also an ambassador for resurrection, in that he always had the nerve and skill to believe that everything could be fixed.

Which isn't that far from St Paul's dictum that nothing in all creation, neither life nor death, absolutely nothing, is beyond the love of God in Christ Jesus our Lord. And that includes votive stands and Austin Sevens brought back to life by the best priest Helmsley never had!

I like to take out home communions on Maundy Thursday; one or two of my communicants were in a bad way, and it could well be their last Last Supper. My first port of call was Norman, a guy I always adored visiting, because his little flat was a veritable shrine to the railway age. Bradshaw's guides from way-back-when were piled up like towers, the walls were festooned with paintings of steam trains, shelves and ledges were crammed with Hornby 00 engines and carriages: visiting him was a sheer feast for a railway amateur like me.

This morning the nurse had got there before me and was bathing and dressing Norman's ulcerated legs and feet, kneeling before him with a bowl of water and a towel, an apron wrapped around her uniform. It was the most arresting of sights on Maundy Thursday of all days, the day when Christ humbly stooped to wash his disciples' feet. 'Do you realise the significance of doing that on this particular day,' I asked the nurse, as I sat in a chair, engines and carriages littering each arm.

'Of course I do,' she replied, quite huffily, 'my mother's a priest!'

'Erm, you don't sound very pleased about it, if you don't mind me saying,' I replied, feeling brave in the face of her brusqueness.

'Well, no, I'm not pleased to be honest. In the good old days, before she got ordained, mum used to cook the whole family the most marvellous Sunday lunch. Now that she's taking services here, there and everywhere on a Sunday, we're lucky if she makes us a sandwich.'

I laughed. Of the many arguments I had heard against women priests (mostly misogynism in a velvet glove) hers was the only one that seemed to carry any water. And as I watched her wash Norman's feet with the greatest of tenderness, I could see where her mother had got her priestliness from. As they say, 'Insanity is hereditary: you get it from your children!' So is holiness.

🗨 *Good Friday, 10th April*

Another call I made yesterday on my home communion round was to Betty, wife of Neil the vet and co-director of the Helmsley menagerie. I parked my bike by the heavy lichen-encrusted farm gate that marks the entrance to their spacious grounds and pushed the gate open, its un-oiled hinges loudly groaning. This attracted attention of the two deerhound 'puppies', who bounded towards me, barking loudly.

Normally I adore dogs and have a good rapport with them, but there was something about these two that was distinctly threatening, so I made a run for the front door at full pelt, flanked by a hound to the right and left of me, each snapping and snarling head level with my shoulder. Neil must have seen my flight and opened the front door, letting me in in the nick of time, before slamming it to thwart my two canine pursuers, who had to apply the tightest of left and right locks to avoid colliding with the house's stone wall. Given their size and speed, I wouldn't have put any money on whether the house or them would have fared worse had they not deftly avoided collision. I had once seen a sparrowhawk pursuing a sparrow. The plucky little bird had flown through a slightly open window, losing a few tail feathers in the tightest of squeezes, but forcing its pursuer to abort its chase and steer the steepest of banks. That little sparrow had my every sympathy.

'They have a thing about men on bicycles!' was Neil's wry comment as he hung up my coat. Clearly some creatures can never forgive their saviour for bringing them life and healing, as Good Friday marks only too well.

I have reflected on this heaviest of days and heaviest of weeks since my early childhood. For my third birthday my parents gave me a wooden jigsaw puzzle. Not for me the delights of piecing together Spot the Dog, or Andy Pandy, or Pooh Bear; for reasons best known to themselves, my parents decided that my first puzzle should be Leonardo da Vinci's *Last Supper*. To make matters worse, my mother laboured under the misconception that the completed puzzle would fit perfectly into the cardboard box it came in, so we duly arranged the edge pieces around the box's perimeter and worked inwards. Since the jigsaw's area was actually slightly smaller than the area of the box, we ran out of pieces before we completed the centre, leaving a great hole in the middle of Jesus' stomach. Not to be outdone, my mother forced into the gap a piece from a cast-off Red Riding Hood jigsaw bound for the jumble sale. The piece didn't quite fit perfectly, nor did the wolf's snout blend into Jesus' tunic as inconspicuously as my mother claimed. Every time I have encountered da Vinci's masterpiece since, I have never quite rid myself of that strange lupine sensation.

Years later some parishioners gathered in our downtown Hull vicarage for drinks on Christmas Eve. They got round to discussing the merits of da Vinci's *Last Supper*, as you do at Christmas in UPAs. 'I've got a picture just like that over our mantelpiece,' one stalwart addressed the increasingly inebriate gathering, 'only, it's with ballet dancers.' We all nodded sagely, having cracked the *Da Vinci Code,* way, way before its time.

Part Three

1998: Easter to Summer

🔖 *Easter Day, 12th April*

Some years back I had been the guest preacher at a Three Hours service for Good Friday at Cottingham, near Hull. I had carefully chosen the hymns and readings and kicked off the proceedings at noon by announcing the first hymn, number 67, 'When I survey the wondrous cross'. Unfortunately they had a different hymnbook with different numbering. Number 67 in their book was 'In the bleak mid-winter', so the congregation looked a bit fazed until their vicar intervened and moved them on from Christmas to Holy Week in the twinkling of an eye.

As I started to cycle the five miles up the cruel 1:3 hills from Helmsley to the highest point on the North York Moors at half past four this morning, 'In the bleak mid-winter' seemed apt and seasonal. Blizzard upon blizzard was blowing in from the North Sea, with snow truly falling snow on snow, crunching crisply under my bicycle wheels as I skidded and weaved from one side of the lane to the other. By the time I had struggled to the top of the first hill, the snow was so deep that you couldn't tell which was road or hedge or field, a polar scene with no landmarks for guidance.

Except one: a hare had clearly ascended the hill just before me and left her tracks in the fresh snow. Some country folklore stirred in the back of my mind about hares having a built-in altimeter which enabled them always to ascend if lost in a blizzard, so since ascending was my objective too, I simply followed her tracks. She didn't let me down, and after an hour I found myself at the very top of the dark North York Moors.

As I brushed the snow off my rucksack and unpacked the paschal candle, robes and orders of service, the voices in my head said that this was all folly, since surely no one else would come to this bleakest of places at such an unholy hour. Indeed my old friends the out-of-work U-boat commanders had been good enough to point out the sheer stupidity of having a dawn service on top of the moors, and that was even before an Arctic blizzard was on the menu. 'Why can't you keep up Vicar Gray's tradition of having the Easter Vigil in church at a civilised hour on Holy Saturday evening, rather than gallivanting off in the middle of the night to an event to which no one will come?' Not that many had come to their event, I had realised, as I flicked through Helmsley's church registers and, noticing the low numbers, planned something a little different this year.

Even so, as I set the paschal candle firmly in the frozen earth, donned my white robes and shivered, I prepared myself for a solitary celebration. But then I looked back towards Helmsley through the billowing blizzard, and gasped with what breath remained as I saw a train of headlights: car upon car was labouring up the moors to join me. Four-by-fours galore circled me like a wagon train protecting itself against a Red Indian attack, their warmly wrapped-up drivers and passengers and even a dog or two alighted and slithered on the ice, wishing me a cheery good morning and Happy Easter. We began our service while it was yet dark, then pitch black turned to a murky grey and an Easter Day Yorkshire panorama, fifty miles wide, dawned before our peering eyes, as the snow cleared and the sun rose over the North Sea, thirty miles away. Many of the thirty-five folk who had joined me rarely if ever came to church. I wondered for a moment if I was tapping into something primitive: was I a minister of Christ's resurrection or was I a rallying point for something more sinister? Was this simply a gathering of the secret devotees of the gods of high places, including El and his sidekick Baal, whom the philandering Israelites had worshipped when they fancied not so much a bit on the side but a god on the side? But then a shepherd boy joined us on his quad bike, turned off his roaring engine and took off his baseball cap in respect. And I was comforted as I thought of another shepherd boy, another David, who saw off the false gods of the Philistines in favour of the one true God.

And as everyone trilled 'Jesus Christ is risen today' with all their heart and soul, mind and strength, I realised I was amongst the truly faithful, for whom going to a cosy church was too easy an option compared to scaling a mountain of ice.

To make sure the paschal candle ignited in a blizzard, on the previous day I had scooped out balls of wax from around the wick, filled the cavity with cotton wool and then soaked it with meths prior to our service, with the result that the candle blazed like a rocket. At the end of our service I looked beyond Helmsley to the Yorkshire Wolds twenty-five miles to the south. There in the distance I noticed another flame, and realised it was my good friend, Michael, who had dragged his congregation to the top of his hills to greet the sunrise on the day the Son rose.

I took the long route home, cycling along the bank top and then dropping into Helmsley via a snowy Rievaulx, realising that these were the views of a lifetime.

There's something within me that adores pitching just myself and my bicycle against the wildest conditions, which I guess was set in boyhood. Our tiny village school had been addressed by the last surviving member of Shackleton's Antarctic Expedition of 1914–15. This Ancient of Days, decked in a moth-eaten woolly jumper which smelt strongly of fish, had shown us his glass slides on his magic lantern: their ship the *Endurance* crushed by pack ice and sinking; the bleak Polar landscape where they sheltered beneath upturned lifeboats for five months, surviving on a diet of penguin and seaweed; the inhospitable cliffs of South Georgia, which Shackleton and five others had to scale before they could summon rescue. But more than those haunting pictures, I recall the tale of how every time they did a head count, they always felt there was one more member in addition to their twenty-nine-strong party: Christ the thirtieth man, straying from Emmaus for an Antarctic sojourn. I had no doubt that he proved the thirty-eighth man to join our near Antarctic sojourn today.

Just to check my memory wasn't playing tricks, just before Easter I rang my old headmaster to check all the detail, or had my hyperactive imagination dreamt the whole school visit? 'Oh yes, he was called Green,' he confirmed. 'He must have been in his eighties and he insisted on coming all the way from Hull on public transport, struggling with his magic lantern and heavy glass slides. I'd offered to pick him up, but he'd have none of it. Absolutely incredible!' I did point out that if someone had rowed 800 miles across the frozen Southern Ocean, then perhaps even a 30-mile bus journey from darkest Hull would hold no fears.

🍂 *Sunday, 19th April*

At this time of the year the rising sun makes Christ the King truly dazzle in our Te Deum East Window, surrounded by adoring trios of prophets, martyrs, apostles, etc. This morning, as the sun highlighted the midriffs of the company of virgins directly below Jesus, I suddenly realised that each stomach was well rounded with the bloom of pregnancy. Was this symbolic, were they virgin-bearers of the Word? Or was the artist having the last laugh at the expense of Charles Gray, my Victorian predecessor, who fiercely eradicated promiscuity throughout the town only to find it beaming at him from his precious stained glass?

The sun shining through the dubious virgins in the East Window reminded me of an ingenious theory I had come across about the origin of crooked chancels. Far from being the result of sloppy workmanship, such architectural oddities arose out of an obsessive desire to make sure the church pointed due east, marked by the position of the rising sun on the particular church's patronal day. Because of the Julian calendar's being slightly out of phase, when there was a considerable interval between one stage of building and the next, the sun would rise at a slightly different point, albeit on the same calendar day. Faced with this disparity, the architect would doggedly make the church crooked, rather than condemn the latest edition to be obviously out of ecclesiastical alignment.

Moved though I was by the devotion of a previous age to kneeling in the right place and direction when the Son of Man came again (like lightning, from the east), one or two points in the theory made me wonder. Such as what happened when the patronal day dawned overcast. Was it a case of 'Down your tools lads, we'll just have to wait until this time next year. And for God's sake, pray for sunshine!'

Or was the particular festal day decided when the rising sun deigned to show herself? 'Quick, get up and fetch the masons – the sun's peeping on the horizon. And while you're about it, go and kick the parish priest out of bed and ask him which saint's day it is!'

Such dialogue sounds almost as implausible as Ken Follett's *The Pillars of the Earth,* yet it would go a long way towards explaining some peculiar dedications in these cloudy parts.

Sunday, 2nd May

I find conducting the 8am Communion on a Sunday an increasingly eerie experience. I'm not sure why, when I have been a devotee of the slot for over thirty years – after all Mary Magdalene set the precedent for getting up early on the first day of the week, while it was yet dark, to meet her Lord. I guess in my early, nervous days of ministry the form of service suited me well. I wasn't expected to say or do anything, other than get my tongue around the set Elizabethan words and actions. And facing eastwards at the altar, I could turn my shy back on my audience, who had that eyes-staring-straight-ahead look that commuters reserve for buskers on tube stations, as if what I was doing had nothing to do with them anyway.

But now that look disturbs me as I try, unsuccessfully, to disarm it with words of welcome and cheery notices. 'Don't bother me with this intimacy stuff,' they seem to be saying, at this, surely the most intimate of services. And when I turn my back and celebrate facing eastwards, I hear feet shuffling and wonder what they are up to, fearing they are playing some macabre version of grandmother's footsteps and are about to mob me. It is always with considerable relief when I turn around and simply find them all kneeling devoutly at the altar rail.

After last week's 8am Sunday Communion, a woman harangued me with the severity of one of Saki's aunts, complaining that our congregation never exceeded a dozen. This Sunday I stood outside the church prior to the early Communion, fearing her wrath once again, praying that today our congregation might at least reach the mid-teens (in number if never in age). Immediately and miraculously two teenage nymphs strode down the path, auburn-haired, vibrant, beautiful. Both had a silver ring on their finger. 'We're from Chicago,' they explained, 'we're spending a year touring Britain, studying English literature. There'll be a few more of us along in a minute.' Sure to form, ten others soon joined them, nine equally stunning girls and one deliriously happy lad.

They proved alert, worked confidently through the maze that is BCP Communion, responding loudly and crisply, putting our usual whispers to shame. Their contagious liveliness moved me to preface the Prayer for the Church with a meditation. That and having to communicate over 25 people meant that we finished about a quarter of an hour later than usual, and the congregation rushed off before their breakfasts spoiled. My critic of the previous week had a look in her eye which spoke mountains: 'Next week, we'll revert to the usual dozen if you don't mind, Vicar.'

My family were just a tad anxious when I returned home late for my breakfast. You don't have to be a Prayer Book Society prize-winner to know that the Lord's Prayer occurs twice in the BCP Communion, once at the beginning and then repeated after the administration. I have always joked with Rachel and the girls about committing a liturgical homoioteleuton, mistaking the second time for the first and beginning the whole service again, condemning me and my communicants to a loop that could go on for ever. 'Where's Daddy?' one of my children would ask as my porridge was going cold. 'Oh goodness me,' my wife would reply, 'he must have got stuck again.' In a scenario that is a cross between *Father Ted* and *Monty Python*, the bishop is summoned, bursts into church and wails, 'Don't say the *Pater Noster*, Vic!' liberating me and my weary congregation from our everlasting liturgy.

Thursday, 7th May

'This church is usually open from 1pm to 6pm every Sunday', the yellowing notice informed me – not much consolation when you're reading it at 12 noon on a Thursday! The place was Goodmanham, 'not far east of York, beyond the River Derwent' (according to the Venerable Bede's gazetteer). It was here that the High Priest Coifi, egged on by Archbishop Paulinus and York's King Edwin, had desecrated his own pagan shrine, overturned its altars and burnt it to the ground. Ever since this colossal act of vandalism, the locals understandably have been a touch jumpy about visitors. Yet my overactive imagination re-ran the episode on a certain Thursday 1380 years ago. Edwin, Paulinus and Coifi make the sorriest return to their ancient palace in Elmet, their stallions sultry. 'My goodness, boys,' Queen Ethelburga greets them, 'that was quick. Desecrating the shrine must have been a pushover!'

'No, it were shut!' Edwin complains, in his native broad Yorkshire.

Fortunately I hadn't journeyed fifty miles just to inspect Goodmanham church. I was addressing the Yorkshire Country-women Association's branch at nearby Market Weighton and, like Bede's trio, felt the heavy hand of history on my shoulder. The event was organised by the wife of the headteacher of the little village primary school I had attended in the 1960s. When I had rung her husband out of the blue just before Easter to check my Shackleton story, she had been keen to book me for her YCA programme. Now both she and her husband were in the audience, and as we chatted afterwards we easily bridged the four decades since our last meeting.

We recalled a marvellous nativity play the school had staged at the local church in 1966. It was traditional and epic – in order to involve every child in the 90-strong school the script began with Isaiah and followed through the eight centuries to Christmas. I, as the school's head boy, had been tipped to be the play's narrator, but my unfortunate boyhood habit of failing to roll my *r*s prevented me. This Jonathan Ross of a vicar's son proclaiming 'The angel Gab*w*iel came into her *w*omb and said …' would have been too novel a take on the incarnation, even for the radical 1960s. So instead I was cast as Joseph, which suited me just fine, since the prettiest head girl was cast as Mary: Christmas truly came early for me that year.

A photo was shown around the packed YCA meeting of a very hot me, decked in my father's dressing gown, with false beard and moustache gingerly held on by spirit-gum. Tied around my head was a towel, whose gaudiness was undiminished even by the black and white photo – I was Joseph and the Amazing Technicolor Tea-towel a year before Andrew Lloyd Webber's Joseph took the world by storm. Beside me was Mary, looking olive-skinned and Semitic, with a gaze into the distance which was positively beatific. She went on to be one of the world's top fashion and style experts, so maybe she was looking into the happiest future.

My headteacher recalled how a door had opened and let the future in for me too. Under the hot spotlights at the play's dress rehearsal he was getting really wound up and shouting at the cast for their poor diction. Suddenly I, a Joseph definitely out-of-role, tapped him on his shoulder and pleaded, 'Smile, sir, you're on *Candid Camera*!'

Until he reminded me, I had entirely forgotten that episode, but then the memories came flooding back. My sense of upset that the man who was my hero and role model was getting stressed; my sense of risk that the stunt I planned could go either way and either disarm the situation or escalate it; my sense of shyness that I could all too easily blow my crucial punchline. But the ruse worked: Mr Nixon laughed, ruffled my ginger hair and the rehearsal and play that followed went just fine. And ever since then, I guess I've always gone for the funny line, in season and out of season, seeking the humorous in the deadliest of situations; and the Church, God bless her, doesn't half send a lot of dead stuff my way to practise on!

🍂 Sunday, 10th May

Sunday lunch was interrupted by a phone call. 'My sister needs her baby christening NOW!' the caller urgently informed me. I dashed around to the address, and found a plump baby bouncing on her mother's knee, surrounded by a sea of toys, discarded nappies and teething rings, in the rudest of health, definitely not knocking on Limbo's door. Neither mother nor aunt showed signs of any imminent demise nor hellfire conversion, so after half an hour of failing to find any evidence whatsoever why they were in such a rush, I gently asked why the baptism needed to be so soon. 'Why, it's the christening gown,' the sister explained, as if stating the obvious. 'It's a family heirloom and if she puts any more weight on, we'll never get her into it!'

Friday, 15th May

Ryedale School had a taster day today for all the little Year 6s from half a dozen local primary schools on the verge of going up to big school. We aimed to make it all sheer fun for them, tag teams scaling the climbing wall, cathode ray oscilloscopes mapping heart beats, heads of science sparking with ten thousand volts of electrostatic charge, a mini French lesson with a range of tasty French foods provided for a picnic – 'Urgh, what they given me garlic for, I'm not a vampire,' complained one albeit intelligent Francophobe from high on the moors. All topped off with a rounders match between smiling senior staff and sundry Year 6 teams, with every single child a winner.

The sun shone and the day went well: by its end every child had that happy air of expectancy for starting in September that children normally reserve for Christmas Day's dawn. Such a stark contrast to the introduction I had had as a terrified 11-year-old to Archbishop Holgate's Grammar School in York, way back in 1967. All the new boys were herded together the day before term began and sternly lectured on a plethora of rules which would have done Moses proud, a whole host of 'thou shalt nots' with canings and detentions the ultimate deterrents. Three hours of homework each and every evening was to be the norm, and given absolute priority. 'Please, Sir, am I allowed to have my tea?' I asked nervously, really believing that if I didn't ask permission, my form master would burst out of our pantry at home and harangue me for disobeying his orders.

A brief episode at the very beginning of our taster day today, brilliant though it was, had made me recall my 1967 dread. All the Year 6s gathered in the hall and Paul, the Head of Lower School, stood before them. 'Good morning, boys and girls. I am the Head of Lower School, but you can call me sir,' Paul boomed in his best Brian Blessed voice. The 120 Year 6s didn't get his sense of irony, something which tends to go over the heads of most 11-year-olds, so instead they shivered.

All except Laura, star of the *Amazing Technicolor Dreamcoat* and *The Sound of Music*. She broke free of her classmates and teachers and zigzagged towards Paul with a speed which would have made a rugby fly-half proud and simply hugged him. It was truly a 'Goodbye Mr Chips' moment, where the stiff and starched schoolmaster is made warm and human by the love of a good woman. Similarly as Laura wrapped her arms around Paul's legs and he smiled, Paul became warm and human before every Year 6, fierce dictator transformed to tender daddy in front of their very eyes. Laura saved the day. I mentioned back in November that her parents had opted for mainstream education for her: but as in so many situations, it was Laura who educated us.

🍃 Thursday, 21st May

When I worked as Archbishop of York's chaplain, I used to cover occasionally for clergy who were poorly. One Sunday I found myself taking services at the deeply rural parish south-east of York where, thirty years previously, my dad had been vicar. Waiting in the vestry for the service to start, I flicked back through the pages of the service register three decades, until I came across the entries made in my dad's neat handwriting, including one for Holy Communion at 10am on Ascension Day 1967. In the column for the number of communicants were the simple words, 'No one came.'

I imagined my dad, biking the three miles to the little church, casting the words of his little Ascension sermonette as he cycled, unlocking the church, unpacking his robes, painstakingly preparing the altar, ringing the bell, waiting for the rattle of the ancient door handle to signify that at least one other person had kept faith on this most holy of days. Ten o'clock came and went, five past, ten past, then the realisation that no one was coming, putting everything away unused, the bread going back into its Charles Farris tin, the wine back into its bottle, followed by the sorry cycle ride home. Walter de la Mare's poem 'The Listeners' sprang to mind: 'Tell them I came, and no one answered, that I kept my word.'

Ever since then, I have been determined that I was never ever going to write 'no one came' in my church's register for Ascension Day, determined to recover the high profile of this most holy of days using sundry ruses to attract the crowd.

Today's ruse was to get our thirteen-strong church choir to climb with me to the top of the church tower at 7am to sing the Ascension hymn 'Hail the day that sees him rise' to the waking and somewhat startled town. The choir had been rehearsing the choral part of their performance for weeks, but I had been deliberately cagey about the practical side. The easiest part was the eighty steep and narrow spiral steps up to the belfry where Helmsley church's eight bells were hung. Then a climb up a long wooden ladder to a floating platform above the bells, and then up another wooden ladder to an ancient woodworm-infested beam, which ran from one side of the tower to the other, high above the metal bell-frame. Each member of the choir had to crawl along this beam, carefully inch themselves over another beam halfway across, until reaching the trapdoor onto the roof. Beneath the trapdoor's entrance were a couple of handles. These you had to use (with all the dexterity of an Olympic athlete on parallel bars) to swing yourself up before spilling out onto the roof above.

Health and Safety would have had a fit, but whoever said that a Gospel whose heart includes taking up one's cross and following our Lord was either healthy or safe! Some members of my choir were well into their sixties, one or two had a girth which matched if not exceeded the width of the narrow trapdoor, yet all were the best of sports and not only made it to the top, but sung their hearts out for all seven verses accompanied by a cornet player who had shinned up the tower to keep them in tune. Another good sport, the Bishop of Whitby, joined us and said his Ascension Blessing over the town, competing with the Thursday bin lorry which decided to rev its engine in the market place below. About thirty people gathered below the tower to witness the spectacle and then we all adjourned to Canons Garth for croissants and home-made raspberry jam. I proudly wrote in the church register: 46 came; 16 ascended, which should be a real puzzler for any of my descendants who end up taking a service at Helmsley.

Tuesday, 26th May

The Archdeacon rang. They're being very hot on Health and Safety in the diocese at the moment, and driving past Helmsley churchyard on Saturday morning, he'd noticed our gardener cutting the church grass without goggles, ear protectors or a helmet. Keeping shtum about our recent ascent up the tower, I did point out to the archdeacon that had I even dared to suggest to Dennis, our indefatigable gardener, that he don just one of these unmanly items, I'd be the one to need protection, like a latter-day Father Ted wearing body armour to cut Father Jack's nails.

In my over-heated imagination, I back-tracked two millennia and revisited that ominous first day of the week, while it was yet dark, when Mary Magdalene thought her newly risen Lord was the gardener. Maybe it was the goggles, helmet and ear protectors, those *sine qua nons* of responsible after-life, that misled her.

Joking apart, the biblical epics do jar somewhat with a generation prone to cosset itself against every conceivable hazard. What Health and Safety policy would tolerate revelation through cosmic flood or torched bushes or fire-topped mountains or walking on water or drinking from a shared cup? I recently read a book by Annie Dillard called *Teaching a Stone to Talk,* which catches the paradox perfectly:

> On the whole, I do not find Christians, outside of the catacombs, sufficiently sensible of conditions. Does anyone have the foggiest idea what sort of power we so blithely invoke? Or, as I suspect, does no one believe a word of it? The churches are children playing on the floor with their chemistry sets, mixing up a batch of TNT to kill a Sunday morning. It is madness to wear ladies' straw hats and velvet hats to church; we should all be wearing crash helmets. Ushers should issue life preservers and signal flares; they should lash us to our pews. For the sleeping god may wake someday and take offence, or the waking god may draw us out to where we can never return.

🔖 Whit Sunday, 31st May

The joke about the elderly peer having the nightmare that he was making a speech in the House of Lords, and waking up to find that he was, proved more than a bit close for comfort today. My recurrent nightmare on Saturday night is that I stand inappropriately clad, if clad at all, before my congregation. My palms sweat, my fingers fumble through the Prayer Book, turning up the Burial of the Dead rather than Holy Communion. After what seems an age, I find the correct place, but then the words dance around the page, like frisky steers resolutely refusing a halter. After another aeon, I manage to lasso a phrase with a gaze which is positively laser in intensity, but then my voice squawks like a cockatoo.

Most clergy suffer from such nightmares, primarily because leading an Act of Worship aimed at the immortal, invisible God of the Big Bang, dinosaurs and all stops in between is bound to be a tad stressful. Recent research came up with the conclusion that just speaking in public (let alone speaking in public to God) is more stressful than dying. I don't know quite how they gathered in their data, but certainly when I preach at a funeral, I do feel I am going through more than the corpse in the cosy coffin lying before me. When I was first ordained I feared, from the grim look of a congregation at a funeral, that they were angry over something I had said; it was only experience that made me realise that they were not angry at me, but angry with grief and loss.

Today my nightmares were made flesh. Taking my cue from liberation brought by the first Pentecost, I was trying to free up our regular Sunday Eucharist by taking a leaf from John Robinson's book, *Liturgy Coming to Life*. The book records how, as a dean of a Cambridge college, Robinson attempted to root Communion in every day stuff, with 'bread baked in the college ovens, wine from the college cellar'. I had urged Julia, our sidesperson for today, to bake a bread bun and buy half a bottle of red wine. My new churchwarden's shop sells a decent claret with a screw cap which is perfect for the purpose, and far better than the sickly sweet communion wine we normally endure – I for one prefer not to greet my Saviour with a wince!

Julia's two toddlers joined her for the offertory procession, and looked so sweet until the younger of them had second thoughts about presenting me with the prized bread bun baked by his mum, and ran off with it. 'I'm afraid the bread's gone walkabout,' I joked as I chased him around the pulpit. Eight American visitors guffawed loudly. His sister was more staid and presented me solemnly with a wine bottle. But rather than the usual screw top, I was aghast to discover it had a cork. 'What am I supposed to do with this,' I blurted out to her mother. 'Oh, I'm so sorry,' Julia replied, 'I didn't realise you wanted to open it now!' What else she thought I was planning to do with it escaped me. But as it happened she had a Swiss Army knife in her handbag with a corkscrew attachment. Unfortunately all this stress had made my hands too sweaty to get some torque on the cork, so instead I handed the bottle to my ever-cool churchwarden, who immediately extracted the cork with a loud pop. The eight Americans clapped and cheered loudly, pleased that at least one Brit wasn't as uptight as they had been led to believe; an impression unfortunately not corroborated by the black looks in their direction from distinctly unmoved locals.

As I tried to recover my composure, following the offertory I was a little too enthusiastic with the censer, and bashed it against the altar. A cloud of sparks flew out, descending like a mini-meteorite shower on the sanctuary carpet. I deftly kicked the blazing charcoal onto the stone flags, stamping out the smouldering Axminster while the bemused congregation wondered at my novel liturgical dance.

Calm returned and I proceeded with the Eucharistic Prayer, though puzzled that the smog seemed to be thickening rather than clearing. Then during the Sanctus I spotted smoke rising from the collection plate on the altar – a red-hot charcoal tablet had landed in its middle and was chewing its fiery way through a bunch of planned-giving envelopes, leaving a perfect circular hole in each before dropping down to the next one. I hastily picked up the plate and took it into the vestry, where the thurifer was lurking, doing what thurifers do. 'Put this out please,' I requested. As he took the thing off me, he bowed with his usual reverence.

Our fire officer is also a chalice assistant, so when he came up to the altar at the administration I reported the incident to him, *sotto voce*. Instead of checking the area out for any other blazing coals we might have missed, he was overcome by giggling of an intensity not usually witnessed in the hallowed confines of Helmsley's church. Mind you, the collect for the day had prayed that the Holy Spirit would be the life and *light* of the Church, so perhaps God was giggling too. Especially as the offertory hymn had been 'O thou who camest from above, the fire celestial to impart …'.

Not that we sang it without considerable competition. As the hymn came to its close, the distant strains of a marching band grew louder and louder. I crooned the Communion preface at maximum volume while the wretched band encircled the church, but realised even my booming bass couldn't compete. I soon found I was taking my key from the band's rendering of 'Yellow submarine', investing it with some novel ecclesiastical lyrics which almost perfectly fitted Lennon and McCartney's metre: 'In the town, where I was born … therefore with angels and archangels.' By the time we reached the Sanctus the Scout band had thankfully marched on to disrupt worship at the Methodist chapel, and me and our broadly grinning congregation were firmly back on Merbecke's line, not too unnerved at having the world's tune imposed on our little Eucharist.

It's not the first time I've leapt from one tune to another. My *bête noire* is the funeral hymn, 'The old rugged cross', which in an unguarded moment I tend to merge with Tom Jones' sixties' hit, 'The green, green, grass of home'. 'On a hill, far away, stands an old … town looks the same, as I step down from the train, and there to greet me are my momma and my poppa.' In my worst nightmare, mourners give me a pitying, bewildered look; although fortunately I am obviously not quite a dead ringer for Tom Jones, in that they have yet to hurl their underwear at me. Never mind the underwear: bread buns, corked wine and red-hot charcoal tablets are more than enough to cope with.

🔖 *Wednesday, 3rd June*

Betty, the woman who had regaled me with her railway tales from wartime Helmsley, was seriously ill in York District Hospital. She'd had a hard life but also a fantastic life, and now she was simply worn out. Her bed was by the window and I sat by her bedside holding her hand, neither of us saying anything. Instead we both looked out of the window at York Minster's grandeur, which heartened me and heartened her. 'It's simply marvellous,' she said. And those were her last words to me.

My own love affair with York Minster began in 1962 when, as a very bewildered child of six, I entered the Minster with my mother and watched my father ordained deacon and priest. Twenty years later I returned, no less bewildered, to be ordained deacon and priest myself. I felt very unworthy both for the ministerial office and also to be centre of stage in this magnificent building which dominates York's skyline.

When my father was ordained priest he bought me a present, a book entitled *Nick and Cecilia in York Minster,* whose eponymous heroes have a holiday with their uncle, the Canon in residence, and pore over the Minster's treasures. For many years it was my favourite book – you realise what a wildly exciting childhood I had – although reading some of its twee lines now makes my toes curl. Such as: 'The children had never been to a service in the Minster before, but they were not too young to appreciate its beauty and its dignity.' Dream on: my very bored 4-year-old daughter fell soundly asleep when I first preached in York Minster! But the book concludes with a gnostic comment, '"We'd have missed quite a lot of the Minster if you hadn't shown us round," said Nick. '"You have to learn how to look," said his uncle, "and that doesn't come all at once," and he smiled as he walked away.'

Since 1962 I have been learning how to look at York Minster. My boy's heart missed a beat when they launched the six-million-pound appeal to save the central tower in the 1960s. To a boy whose father earned £6 a week as a curate, six million pounds was an impossible amount and I thought the Minster was doomed. I remember York College for Girls, whose premises were in the shadow of that tower, had an emergency meeting with parents to discuss what they could do should the tower fall on them. Not a lot, really. As Flanders and Swann quipped about Low Flying Aircraft signs: 'Not a lot you can do about that, other than take your hat off!'

I planned on doing more than that. I was quite keen on one of the girls at York College. My own school was Archbishop Holgate's Grammar, which had wisely relocated a safe two miles away from the Minster. In my boyhood fantasy as soon as I heard the rumble, heralding the central tower's imminent collapse, I would shin the two miles down the Hull Road and drag to safety my puppy love, who would be eternally grateful to me for saving her from being killed by a cathedral.

Whatever, the money was raised and the tower was saved. For the next few years a trip to Evensong was sexed up by watching the underpinning of the tower, complete with its own railway conveying stone and iron rods and cement into the bowels of the earth, the rattle of the trucks a novel accompaniment to *Darke in F.*

I felt physically sick when the south transept roof was gutted by fire in 1984, as if a part of me was burnt. Surely this was the end? And yet once again York Minster rose from the ashes, more glorious, a superb visual aid of resurrection.

Shortly after the fire, I took a parish trip to York from Middlesbrough and we parked in Lord Mayor's Walk. 'Which way's the Minster?' a hapless parishioner asked me. 'Look up,' I said, trying not to sound too exasperated. Because the Minster is unmissable, a sign of the infinite in the midst of the finite. It dominates York, boldly and breathlessly, the rest of York's buildings are mere chicks compared to the Minster's huge mother hen. Far away up Garrowby Hill on the road to Bridlington, the Minster still looms on the horizon twenty miles to the west. Kilburn's White Horse, twenty miles to the North of York, can still see it with its one good eye.

I have been into York Minster's heart for countless services. As Archbishop's chaplain we'd be going there virtually weekly, yet no occasion ever bored me, even a Mothers' Union service where the congregation were instructed to stand tall like stalks of corn and wave in the breeze. On the service sheet was the rubric, 'Congregation to make wind noises', which mercifully they ignored! From consecrations of bishops, to the ordination of the first women priests, to David Hope's enthronement and every stop in between – all brilliant occasions, deserving of Betty's accolade: simply wonderful.

York Minster and its diocese seem to run through my very veins. I was once looking at a road atlas of Yorkshire, and realised I knew virtually every single road in the York Diocese.

Wherever I go in this diocese, I never seem to be more than three miles from a previous parish that either my father or I have ministered in. The ultimate example was when I was travelling with John Habgood across a bleak, wintry North York Moors on our way to a confirmation. An old lady suddenly appeared ahead of us, struggling against the blizzard. 'Stop the car, Gordon, we must give her a lift,' the Archbishop ordered, breaking our usual rule of absolute silence when in transit. The surprised woman was bustled in, and our journey recommenced. 'Let me introduce ourselves,' announced the unusually genial John Habgood, brushing the blown-in snow off his cassock. 'I'm the Archbishop of York.'

'Ooh,' the old lady cooed.

'And the person driving is Gordon my chauffeur.'

'Ooh,' she repeated, suitably impressed.

'And sitting next to him is David, my chaplain.'

'Yes, I know,' she confidently replied. 'I used to look after him when he was a baby.'

Thursday, 11th June

I cycle to a moorland vicarage for a meeting between the local clergy, the Bishop of Whitby and the Archdeacon, an annual visitation when the Establishment try to gee up the troops. Following Communion, each of the clergy present gave a five-minute account of their stewardship. One or two clergy whom I'd assumed had been dead for years suddenly were very much alive, proving the power of the resurrection! They clearly existed in a parallel universe from mine, brimful of tales of gospel heroism, where they prayed for hours before it was yet dawn prior to visiting sundry parishioners before breakfast. Following a breakfast that consisted of little more than a stale crust, they went on to produce their award-winning parish magazine single-handedly, before completing a fun-packed morning by distributing a nutritious lunch (cooked by an equally omnipotent Mrs Vicar) to the housebound.

I decided not to join in this game of ecclesiastical one-upmanship and instead tried to debunk the whole thing by describing my ministry as prowling around like a ravenous lion, desperately seeking any humorous or poignant situation I can write about. The bishop laughed, but some of my colleagues looked shocked — since the aforementioned descriptions of their ministry had clearly belonged to the 'outstanding work of fiction' category, I could hardly see how they could be so scathing about my literary endeavours.

As I huffed and puffed back over the high moor, startled sheep and lambs dived for cover as my bike sliced through their path. Then I came face to face with a fox, only yards away from me. His fur red and sleek, his snout white, his steely gaze bore into my eyes, as if to say, 'Look here, chum, I'm the one who's supposed to scatter the flock; you're supposed to be like the Good Shepherd. Get your role right!' And with that he slunk away to his lair; and I slunk away back to Helmsley.

As the iconic castle came into view, I chanced upon a happier pastoral scene, a shepherd serenely watching his flock. 'What are you up to, John?' I enquired.

'I'm just deciding which sheep to slaughter,' he grinned. Some sheep wisely hid themselves in forlorn and faraway corners. Others tried to look very thin. Others looked indispensable, better alive than dead. A few, foolishly confusing the trophy of privilege with the cup of suffering, bleated 'Pick me, pick me!' It was strangely reminiscent of my earlier meeting at that moorland vicarage. Instead of the shepherd I saw a bishop, instead of sheep, clergy.

We host the bishop for tea — just to prove what a new man I am, and how much in touch I am with culinary fashion, I cook him a *Two Fat Ladies'* recipe of chicken breast dowsed in butter. It all proves a bit too rich, and as butter runs down both our chins, we both nurse the same nostalgic look, yearning for the days when men mercifully were kept out of the kitchen. The bishop is weary of James Cook, having preached no less than eleven sermons on him at anniversaries throughout the arch-deaconry, and feels he can say no more. I sympathise; many clergy haven't even got eleven sermons about Jesus Christ.

Following tea, he and the archdeacon hold an evening meeting for laity in the upper room of Helmsley's Town Hall, normally the quietest of places. But unfortunately this is the night the fair is in town, and the gravity-defying human spinner reaches its maximum 5G thrust at the exact level of the town hall's upper windows. So as its passengers make bulging eye contact with the bishop and archdeacon they shriek in abject terror. Not quite the meeting anyone had in mind.

🍃 *Monday, 15th June*

I am one of the random few to receive a lengthy questionnaire probing into the pastoral care of the clergy. Twenty-seven times it seeks to assess the quality of care extended by my long-suffering bishop. Even Jesus only asked Peter three times if he loved him; twenty-seven times smacks of an interrogation which would make even the most ardent bishopophile crack and in desperation tick the *I hate him* box.

Even twenty-seven versions of the same question are not enough to fill the questionnaire's twenty-eight pages, which soon drift to other fascinating subjects such as praying for the Queen and Prime Minister, as well as probing my psyche. I consistently denied that my mother was strict, distant, unin-volved, uncaring, insensitive, unsupportive, never there, judgemental, selfish, unloving, critical, rejecting and ungiving. I was glad they didn't ask me the same questions about God, although they did ask me whether I felt positively or negatively about my relationship with a) my bishop and b) Jesus. If you answer VP (very positively) to the former, can you answer VnP to the latter, I wondered, with n = infinity?

Did I feel positively or negatively about a) getting practical help in the parsonage garden and b) my reliance on the Holy Spirit? Another curious juxtaposition notwithstanding, what precisely constitutes *impractical* horticultural help? A Church Council working party rolling up? I pondered hard over whether I usually let myself go at a lively party, could easily get some life into a rather dull party and could get a party going: was there some sub-agenda here about my lack of enthusiasm for 8am celebrations?

My number of traumatic events as a minor soared off the Richter scale – you were clearly supposed to tick just one of a) moving more than twice, b) going to a private school, and c) being hospitalised, whereas I scored all three in one go, knocked down by a motor bike coming home from school a few weeks after my parents had flitted yet again. As my fragile psychological state dawned on me, when asked on page 20 if I had experienced suicidal thoughts since ordination, I felt duty bound to reply, 'not until I read this questionnaire!'

◗ *Friday, 19th June*

A mother and toddler queued ahead of me at our local super-market. The little girl obviously took a shine to me and chatted animatedly. It was all total gibberish, but I smiled in response and nodded and tried to look as if I understood. Inwardly I congratulated myself on projecting an image of ministry where even timid little children could see you as their friend. 'She doesn't usually talk to anyone, she's so shy,' her mother explained, further bolstering my clerical ego. 'But I guess she thinks you're Laa-Laa from the Teletubbies in that yellow kagoul.' So much for priestly presence.

Pride pricked, I cycled over to the little convent at Rievaulx and exchanged my yellow kagoul for a white robe and stole. Our regular Friday Eucharists have succeeded beyond Alpha proportions with a 400% increase in attendance: in the small chapel that overlooks the Abbey church, the congregation of three has mushroomed to one of twelve. Strangely none of them comes from our parish. All the twelve are women, who cross half of Yorkshire to be in Rievaulx at noon on Fridays. Most of those women don't feel easy about attending the main Sunday service at their local church, either because they have been bereaved and just don't fancy the hustle and bustle of a normal Sunday, or because they have been damaged, either by the world or by the Church. Whatever, they all feel safe with the quiet Rievaulx sisters, who allow them simply to be themselves before God.

Today I sat in silence at the beginning of the service. 'I'm just waiting for the Vicar of Hovingham and God to turn up before we begin,' I jested, mindful of Desmond Tutu's critique of the Church of England, that she always started her services on time, even if the Holy Spirit hadn't arrived. But once the Vicar of Hovingham had arrived, we duly started. Unfortunately Sister Bridget Mary, a nonagenarian who was just a little hard of hearing, had misheard me say God, and assumed I was referring to a mortal latecomer, named Gord or something. So every time the rustling wind rattled the door, the service was punctuated by her popping out to see if Gord had arrived. I suppose I should have prefaced the *sursum corda* with 'Gord is here!' Except her anxiously peering out for God had an eloquence of its own that I didn't want to curb. Someone once told me that whenever they hold a service in Orthodox Judaism, they always set a man outside the door of the synagogue to look out for the messiah, which seems the most numinous of activities.

Sister Bridget Mary was a fantastic nun, who on her fort-night's annual leave thought nothing of visiting her nephew and niece in Peru, scaling the Andes with them like a mountain goat and returning with the photos to prove it. As a girl she had attended the school in Whitby run by the sisters, and then at eighteen had professed her life vows, just before the Second World War began. At the beginning of the Great War, a German destroyer had shelled Whitby, damaging the abbey and several houses in the town, so the seaside resort was a bit jumpy that history might repeat itself, and the sisters considered relocating their school inland.

But then, as the threat of Nazi invasion of the whole of Britain loomed in the spring of 1940, the sisters proposed a more drastic evacuation. Bridget Mary, who was by then a popular teacher at the school, was assigned the task of single-handedly taking the girls by train to Liverpool and then sailing with them over an Atlantic criss-crossed with U-boats to the safe shores of Canada. The nuns, like most of the British populace, really believed that invasion was inevitable, and felt that sending the girls to Canada would enable this bloom of British maidenhood to be preserved intact until the Nazis were vanquished and it was safe to return. It was a veritable flight to Egypt until the Herodian tyranny was overpast. Bridget Mary, a truly action-nun, often talked breathlessly of the whole esca-pade, but in the same matter-of-fact way that teachers these days talk of a trip to Alton Towers.

◖ Sunday, 21st June

The after-service care was high: wine and eats around the tiny church in the hilltop hamlet of Sproxton as the midsummer sun set, with the Archbishop of York circulating amongst the crowd, celebrating 125 years since the church was moved. This wasn't marking some sort of religious revival that was staged during the mid-Victorian era, but was harking back to the occasion when the church, originally built during the Commonwealth, was moved stone by stone from one hilltop to another. All this was done at the behest of Lord Feversham's ancestor, who fancied moving the little church nearer the edge of his estate, with the strange idea that having a church in their midst would make his estate workers both more moral and biddable.

The conversations over the eats had that forced air which the presence of a Primate induces: I overheard my churchwarden and Lord Feversham discussing the Old Testament, like two delegates at a Torah symposium. 'I find I can't take the gory bits,' my churchwarden confided. She had recently lent me a stomach-turning tome on the myriad diseases afflicting sheep, so I knew she knew what she was talking about. 'Oh, it's the gory bits that make the Old Testament for me,' his Lordship chortled, 'I find I can't get enough of them.'

For a moment Saki's mischievousness became my cue, as I imagined myself as King David, my Old Testament namesake, ransacking his Lordship's parkland, putting his flocks to the sword (employing the helpful hints available in the aforementioned ovine guide), torching his Neo-Gothic mansion and carrying off his fragrant lady. 'No more gory bits, I beg you,' his Lordship pleads, as me and my 600-strong band of Middle Eastern marauding roughs galloped off down his drive.

You see, Saki's short stories unleash a powerful hold on me, with his Edwardian era and my own world often in conjunction, tempting my ministry towards a Saki-like twist. For instance, bored by a Church Council discussion about the launch of a new Sunday School, I found myself musing on the Schartz-Metterklume method of teaching children by making them understand history by acting it out themselves. Championed by Saki's Lady Carlotta, her brief career as a governess comes unstuck when her aristocratic charges act out too literally the rape of the Sabine women, almost violating the gamekeeper's daughters, who have Sabinity unwittingly thrust upon them.

As a naive student on placement in East Leeds, I embraced the method equally as briefly. Encouraging the church children to perform the parable of the Good Samaritan, I stupidly cast some rather rough boys as the thieves: they stole the show, tumbling down the aisle together with the wounded Jew, the Levite, the Priest, the eponymous Samaritan, the Samaritan's donkey and the innkeeper in a rolling ball of fists and boots.

Not to be outdone, the vicar acted out the parable of the houses built on sand and rock, employing a pack of cards, a tray and a large jug of water, visual aids mercifully not available to Jesus. Placing some sand in the tray, he built a house of cards which refused to be shifted, despite the increasing violence with which he rained down water upon them. With his first house still standing, he built a second house of cards on a stone slab, which infuriatingly collapsed as soon as he moved the jug towards it. What moral did those confused children take away? Thank God that none of them grew up to build Barratt Homes; or perhaps they did.

Saturday, 27th June

Every year, one of quiet Helmsley's summer weekends is disturbed by a Motor Cycle Convention. Thousand upon thousand of bikes roar into town, their riders looking like extras from Mad Max movies, scowling at any timid locals who scuttle across their path. They clear the local Co-op's shelves of alcohol

and condoms before disappearing into the depths of Duncombe Park to encamp for a couple of nights. The local folklore
about what precisely goes on there is rich, with tales of lusty
bare-breasted maidens, despairing of their Hells Angels' endless
prattle about pistons and full throttles, instead seducing hapless
locals who stray into their camp. Another narrative attempts to
reassure perplexed locals that most of the bikers are actually
dentists or solicitors, simply taking time out to indulge their
motorcycle hobby. I have come across a fair few dentists and
solicitors in my time, but none has sported whole-body tattoos
or been quite as pierced as these guys.

There wasn't a lusty maiden, nor bare breast, nor dentist, nor
solicitor to be seen when I chanced upon their camp today
when my daughters and I were exercising a parishioner's border
terrier. As we descended down a steep path, the normally
deserted meadow by the shy River Rye looked like a gigantic
sheet of bubble wrap, punctuated as it was with circular tents in
regimented order. We tiptoed over guy ropes which festooned
the meadow like spiders' webs, deafened by the two live rock
concerts being simultaneously staged, each vying with the
other for decibels. The heavy scent of kebab bars and burger
joints ousted the subtle odour of summer grasses and wafted
across the valley.

We witnessed no orgies; the leather-clad bikers stared
through us and gave us no trouble as we gingerly passed their
thousand bedrooms. To them we were invisible, an alien culture
from another time and world, where vicars walked out of an
evening with their daughters and their dogs. 'This is an experience of biblical proportions,' said my daughter, and it suddenly
dawned on me how the ancient peoples of the Middle East
would have felt as they chanced upon the strange hosts of Israel,
encamped on their borders, more numerous than locusts at
plague time. I also wondered about incarnation: and the Word
was made flesh and tripped over our guy ropes.

The waterfalls, which raged like a torrent for most of the year, had all but dried up in the fierce summer sun. We walked across them as if on dry land, the little dog tugging at his lead to chase every darting fish in the stream below. No fierce hoards pursued us, so the waters had no need to close in as we stepped ashore. Perhaps not Exodus after all.

Sunday, 28th June

Often visitors to Helmsley Church feel moved to leave notes, scratched in biro on tatty scraps of paper, with cheery messages such as 'Resign!' or 'Be born again!' or tracts lecturing me on the perils of Catholicism. But before Evensong tonight I discovered this rather sweet little poem perched on my stall:

> Once, when in passion
> of guilt and unbelief
> I turned my thoughts to God on high
> and sought from him relief
> 'My heart is black, my sins are foul,
> of sinners I'm the chief.'
> But my guardian angel, stooping low,
> whispered from behind,
> 'Beware the sin of pride, my son,
> You're nothing of the kind.'

Which reminded me of a story of a teenage girl making her confession. 'Father, I keep staring into the mirror and saying, "Jane, you are beautiful." Is that the sin of pride or vanity?'

'Neither, my dear, just a mistake,' the priest replied, looking lovingly on the rather plain young woman before him.

🍂 *Monday, 29th June*

I awoke at 4.30am with a start, realising I'd forgotten to put the traffic cones out in front of the church for the funeral later that day. With parking spaces in bustling Helmsley at a premium, without the cones the hearse would be forced to double-park. Worse still, it would have to circle the church, like an airliner with fuel gauge veering towards empty, desperately seeking a runway. So I hauled myself out of bed on a distinctly chilly errand.

A light was burning in the butcher's yard opposite the lych-gate, where Ben was already hard at work pressing an ox tongue. He talked animatedly about his New Testament studies, while I nodded sleepily, realising that this was the first and probably the last time in my life I would discuss biblical scholarship at so early an hour.

Churchwarden Ben talks theology in my sleep because he is set to give up his thriving business and pursue a vocation to ordained ministry. While he wants to leave the butcher's to follow his Lord, I realise I've spent a fair bit of my ministry leaving our Lord to hang around butcher's shops. Not only do I adore meat (Ben makes steak pies to die for!) but also I guess I see butcher's shops as holy places of daily sacrifice, where the community gather to be fed. Before Christmas Helmsley holds a competition for the best-dressed shop window. Ben won last December for a brilliant display of hams, pheasant, turkey, geese and mouth-watering pork pies the size of dinner plates. But in the middle of the display was a simple wooden crib full of straw beneath which were written the words, 'Jesus, born in a stable: be the guest at our table.'

If I was trendy, I would call my encounters with butcher's shops 'Fresh Expressions of Church' and apply for a grant from the Archbishop of Canterbury. As it is, I simply let their wooden slabs, stained by real flesh, inform my whiter-than-white altar where I too deal in body and blood.

Mr Dixon, our butcher at Bishopthorpe, was older than Methuselah. One wild, stormy autumn night, he knocked on our door, his wiry frame dressed in the thinnest of overcoats. 'I've come to apologise,' he explained, 'I charged you for stewing steak instead of shin beef. So here's the 17p I owe you.' I guess he belonged to an age when short-changing an archbishop's chaplain by 3/5d was an excommunicable offence.

I revered old Mr Dixon, because, though a staunch Methodist, he had exercised more influence over the Church of England in the twentieth century than any other man. Having provided meat for every Archbishop of York since Lang, he had the heady power to make successive Primates of England contented or dyspeptic. By a strange quirk, Lang, Garbett, Coggan and Habgood, who invariably had sent the cook, the sister, the wife, the boy (i.e. the chaplain) for their order, had alternated with Temple, Ramsey, Blanch and Hope, who had come in person. If this is a definite trend, leave aside the speculation over whether the next Archbishop of York should be Evangelical or Catholic, orthodox or liberal, gay or straight. To fit Mr Dixon's century-long pattern, his only qualification will be that he'll be makkelophobic (Greek for morbid fear of meat markets).

One of Mr Dixon's assistants was a young lad who, like Ben, went for a career change, giving up butchering to raise his son, born blind. Eighteen months later I came across him again when I was a guide at a Bishopthorpe Palace open day and he was visiting with his boy. Neither of us had the vocabulary to describe Bishopthorpe's teeming river or blooming rhododendrons to a child without sight, an awkwardness compounded by an aura of sadness that the young butcher would never be able to pass his trade on to his heir. Sometimes the call is to leave all, yet have nothing to say.

🍂 *Sunday, 5th July*

On this windy Sunday in July, we kept the old feast of the Visitation alfresco in the Cistercian Abbey ruins at Rievaulx. The festival is a trite anachronistic, in that it has John the Baptist leaping in Elizabeth's womb a fortnight after staging his birth, a miracle of obstetrics if ever there was one.

I cycled to Rievaulx Abbey for the early Communion via Duncombe Park, which was hosting a steam fair on a grand scale. A myriad of steam engines huffing and puffing should have been a fitting preparation for visiting a different bygone age at Rievaulx, except there wasn't a single hiss of steam: all the boilers had yet to be stoked and lit. The only sign of life at such an early hour was the lengthy queues for the half dozen portaloos – itself a reminder of clergy conferences of yesteryear before en suites became as prevalent as Eucharists. Two adult deer and their foal that darted across my path tripped another memory: the walls of a former deer park had been ruined by tank manoeuvres during the last war, so that ever since, the deer have roamed free. Steam; cramped clergy gatherings; the war and its aftermath; Rievaulx and its glorious monastic past: memories all subsumed by a liturgy focusing on the greatest memory of them all.

Towards the end of the Communion, instead of saying the Gloria, I asked the congregation simply to turn east and listen to the sounds of the valley, sounds which we would have missed because of our liturgical clamour. The tumbling River Rye, the leaves rustling, the pheasants plaintively calling, the swallows' high-pitched shrieks, the sundry animals: all voicing their Gloria to their creator.

Returning home by another way, I noticed in the distance a massive pall of smoke hanging over the park. The steam engines were now awake and were making their own offering of incense to their creator.

At the actual Eucharist, I found myself preoccupied with stopping the consecrated wafers being blown off the paten by a squall. I wasn't too worried, in that I'd heard of a party visiting the Holy Land who'd held a Communion in a fishing boat on a stormy Lake Galilee. A startled congregation had watched the hosts fluttering across the waters, as a sudden gust of wind blew them all away: Jesus, like football, was coming home. As Southwell Minster's choir sang their plainsong psalms later in Rievaulx's day, so hauntingly and so beautifully, you felt that monasticism was coming home too. In the sixteenth century, Henry VIII's commissioners had been brutal with Rievaulx, tearing the roof down, burning its timbers to ashes, burying the ingots of melted lead deep in the earth, trying to banish worship there for ever. Today worship made a comeback.

🍃 Thursday, 9th July

7am

Ryedale's Head Teacher rings with the tragic news that Paul, Head of Lower School, has died suddenly overnight. I rush around ticking off urgent parish jobs and then cycle into school, collecting my thoughts as I ride.

8.30am

Meet with the Head, Deputy and Head of Music. The school is in the middle of nightly performances of *Grease*, which we decide to continue, provided the cast feel up to it. Paul as Head of Drama was producer of the show.

8.40am

The Head and I break the news at the daily staff briefing. Many weep, unashamedly. As I had come to realise over the last year, Paul was a teacher of intellectual stature, a firm but fair discipli-

narian. My experience, though, is that people with such quali-
ties aren't deeply loved. How wrong could I be!

8.50am

The Head and I break the news to a hastily convened Upper
School Assembly. I end with Cardinal Newman's prayer, 'O
Lord support us all the day long of this troublous life ...' which
I've prayed with every mourning family I've ever encountered.
Many children from this school family are crying. The bruisers,
the bullies, those who look as if nothing could move them are
moved this morning.

9.00am

We break the news to Lower School Assembly. For decades Paul
had managed the transition from Primary School to Secondary
School, aiming to be like a caring father even if he did come
across like Brian Blessed. I talked about another transition, from
life on earth to life with God, and another loving Father.

9.10am

We meet with the cast of *Grease*, distraught and seemingly
inconsolable. This isn't the odd tear-in-the-eye stuff, but body-
wracking sobs. The cast though are unequivocal: they want to
continue with the performance as a tribute to Paul.

10.10am

Most of the cast comes together again for Year 11 Drama, which
the Deputy Head, another teacher and I cover. Those who seem
most distraught I take out to walk around the playing field with
me. The pupils talk openly. Many are in the category 'disaffected
by school' yet voice their gratitude to Paul for keeping them on
board, realising that such care is costly; even, perhaps unto
death.

11.10am

Break. I mingle with staff taking the strain of being strong for the children. I sense the teachers' own grief is complex, including being surprised by how much Paul was loved by his pupils; and by implication how much they are loved.

11.30am

Talk to the Head, who was Paul's neighbour and close personal friend. Interrupted by a heartless phone call from County Hall, asking if we want to stop Paul's pay immediately, or will pay him to the end of the month. Then another call comes from Paul's widow, who asks if I can take his funeral. I agree to preach and manage the tributes, but suggest that the rest of the service is taken by a marvellous retired bishop, who lives in Paul's village.

12.30pm

Lunchtime. The quietest one I have known in any school I have ever been connected with. The Head and I man the reception desk while dictating a letter to be sent home to all parents and governors.

2.30pm

Return to school following a lunch break. Talk with the Admin Staff and then spend a long time in the empty hall with the Head, saying very little.

3.30pm

Meet with the *Grease* cast again to check they still want to go ahead. They do. In a funny way they seem to have cried out their grief.

3.40pm

School ends. I walk through the empty classrooms. Most of the women teachers have gone home. Several men remain at their desks, looking busy, but happy to talk. 'Are you going to *Grease*, then?' I ask the Head of History. 'Well, it is the centre of western civilization, so I feel I really ought to go one day,' he muses. It takes a minute for the penny to drop. 'No, I mean the musical not the country,' I respond, and we both laugh. The first laugh of the day.

6.30pm

Back in school to greet everyone front of house.

7pm

The Head explains to the audience that the show goes on as a tribute to Paul; I then introduce a minute's silence committing Paul to God's gracious mercy; we then launch into *Grease*. The production has a breathtaking energy and talent worthy of a professional theatre company. They certainly did Paul proud. At the end of the play the Head announces that the new theatre suite will be named after Paul. A standing ovation follows.

🍃 *Thursday, 16th July*

Today we buried Paul in the hilltop cemetery at Thornton le Dale. At his funeral Jack, a 15-year-old pupil, gave the perform- ance of his life as he paid his teacher his final tribute. Heather, Paul's colleague, who had been far from well herself, was similarly stunning.

In my sermon I reminded the congregation of the recent Year 6 taster day, with Paul being surprisingly embraced by little

Laura. And then I went a bit mad and asked them to imagine Paul at the gates of heaven like a frightened Year 6 terrified at the prospect of meeting the Ancient of Days, whose gaze was like lightning, whose voice was like thunder, before whom we are all judged and found so wanting. As he stands there shivering, from out of nowhere Jesus runs up and wraps his arms around him, his face radiant, whispering, 'Welcome home'.

🍂 Thursday, 23rd July

Ever since I first saw him on TV in 1976, he has been my companion, staying with me in Hull, Cambridge, Middlesbrough, Pontefract, Bishopthorpe and now Helmsley, bemused by them all. I have visited him in Radnorshire and his native Wiltshire and holidayed with him in Oxford, Wales and Cornwall, where he was a tourist detesting tourists. 'Coming back we met a noisy rabble, rushing down the rocks towards Land's End as if they meant to break their necks − and no great loss either!' This year for our holiday we became tourists in Wensleydale and he reluctantly accompanied us as I re-read him for the umpteenth time. He died 75 years before I was born, but his detailed diary enables us to meet and bounce off each other. His name? The Reverend Francis Kilvert.

I earlier described the cheery confirmation led by the Bishop of Whitby on 25 March. Through my mind's eye, Kilvert watches the bishop eagle-eyed, lest he make the same mistake as the Bishop of Hereford way back in 1870. Taken with 'the new fashion of confirming only two persons at a time, the Bishop mistook a young curate presenting a girl candidate as a candidate himself, and insisted on confirming him. The curate resisted for a long time and had a long battle with the Bishop, but at last unhappily he was overborne in the struggle, lost his head, gave way, knelt down and was confirmed there and then ... with the whole church in a titter.'

With Wensleydale at its hottest, my daughters swam in Redmire Force's deep pools, juxtaposing with Kilvert's experience on Christmas Day 1870 in positively freezing conditions: 'I sat down in my bath on a sheet of thick ice, which broke in the middle into large pieces while sharp points and jagged edges stuck all round the sides of the tub, not particularly comforting to the naked thighs and loins, for the keen ice cut like broken glass.'

Kilvert had trouble with ice, his beard freezing to his mackintosh as he walks to a baptism, baptising the baby 'in ice which was broken and swimming around the font'. I've conducted some odd baptisms, including the one needed urgently before the child outgrew its christening gown, but I have never had to defrost the baby; having to defrost some congregations, on the other hand ...

I sat on a rock, as my daughters continued to swim, an unlikely lifeguard, with Kilvert's Diary perched on my knee. 'Do you allow your daughters to castrate lambs?' Kilvert's ghost asked me, as a stray lamb bleated on the hillside above us. 'Well, the Vicar of Newchurch did. In May 1870 I found the two younger ladies catching and holding the poor little beasts and standing by while the operation was performed, seeming to enjoy the spectacle. It rather gave me a turn of disgust at first ... I don't think the elder members of the family quite expected that the young ladies would be caught by a morning caller castrating lambs, and probably they would have selected some other occupation for them had they foreseen the coming of a guest. However, they carried it off uncommonly well.' I thanked God that my daughters' occupations were more demure; even listening to the Spice Girls pales into insignificance compared to castrating lambs.

With the midday sun blazing, Kilvert is all for bathing naked, tediously moaning about being fettered by swimming costumes. 'At Shanklin one has to adopt the detestable custom of bathing in drawers. If ladies don't like to see men naked, why don't they keep away from the sight? Today I had a pair of drawers given me which I could not keep on. The rough waves stripped them off and tore them around my ankles. While thus fettered I was seized and flung down by a heavy sea, which retreating left me lying naked on the sharp shingle from which I rose streaming with blood. After this I took the wretched and dangerous rag off, and of course there were some ladies looking on as I came out of the water.' I continue to sit tight on my rock, firmly clad.

As I fret that after a year's ministry my Sunday congregations in Helmsley barely total a century, Kilvert reminds me that twenty-nine communicants on Easter Day 1870 was a large congregation. As I recall Richard Conyers, my distinguished predecessor at Helmsley, intimidated by a stranger frowning as he preached, Kilvert too was similarly smitten, commenting that in March 1872 'he could speak much better and more freely when none of the grand people were at church, by reason of the snow.'

To cap it all, Kilvert is an intensely amusing companion. We stare together at an isolated house high in rugged Swaledale. He recalls a Clyro tenant whose complaint that her house was lonely is dismissed by her landlord. 'Lonely indeed! She can see my backdoor.' Kilvert himself enjoys solitude: 'I had the satisfaction of walking from Hay to Clyro by the fields without meeting a single person, always a great triumph to me and a subject for warm self congratulation, for I have a peculiar dislike for meeting people, and a peculiar liking for a deserted road.' I think on the deserted roads on the high moors I have cycled along in my first year in Helmsley and the peace that has met me there.

I think back to the big wedding I took just before our holiday began. The bride had infuriated me, arriving twenty minutes late only to turn in her tracks and retire to the nearby hotel which was hosting their reception to have her mother redo her hair. After a further twenty minutes she reappeared without an apology, with her hair looking worse than it did to start with. Kilvert soothes my ire with the tale of a curate who claimed to be fluent in both Welsh and English. 'Once he was publishing Banns. He meant to say, "… why these two persons may not lawfully be joined together in Holy Matrimony." But what he did say was, "… why these two backsides may not lawfully be joined together in Holy Matrimony." Everyone in Church hid their faces.'

His tedious protests, political incorrectness and grossly inappropriate behaviour frequently make Kilvert's sojourn with us a Strange Meeting. Yet drawing on Wilfred Owen's imagery, Kilvert, in all his blatant transparency, reflects the self I kill by wanting to be thought well of. As Rowan Williams writes in *Open to Judgement*, 'True vocation is when we stop playing games, strip off the veneers and allow ourselves truly to be before God.' Kilvert's chronicles catch that reality and have encouraged me to try and catch mine. Thank you, dear reader, for travelling with me.